SAMS
Teach
Yourself

Ajax

in 10 Minutes

Phil Ballard

SAMS   800 East 96th Street, Indianapolis, Indiana, 46240 USA

Sams Teach Yourself Ajax in 10 Minutes

Copyright © 2006 by Sams Publishing

International Standard Book Number: 0-672-32868-2

Library of Congress Catalog Card Number: 2005934928

Printed in the United States of America

First Printing: April 2006

09   08   07   06   4   3   2   1

Trademarks

Warning and Disclaimer

Bulk Sales

Sams Publishing offers excellent discounts on this book when ordered in quantity for bulk purchases or special sales. For more information, please contact

U.S. Corporate and Government Sales
1-800-382-3419
corpsales@pearsontechgroup.com

For sales outside of the U.S., please contact

International Sales
international@pearsoned.com

ACQUISITIONS EDITOR
Linda Harrison

DEVELOPMENT EDITOR
Damon Jordan

MANAGING EDITOR
Charlotte Clapp

PROJECT EDITOR
Seth Kerney

COPY EDITOR
Geneil Breeze

INDEXER
Ken Johnson

PROOFREADER
Leslie Joseph

TECHNICAL EDITOR
Bill Bercik

PUBLISHING COORDINATOR
Vanessa Evans

MULTIMEDIA DEVELOPER
Dan Scherf

INTERIOR DESIGNER
Gary Adair

COVER DESIGNER
Aren Howell

PAGE LAYOUT
TnT Design

Contents

PART I   A Refresher on Web Technologies

PART II Introducing Ajax

PART III   More Complex Ajax Technologies

PART IV Commercial and Open Source Ajax Resources

About the Author

Phil Ballard graduated in 1980 with an honors degree in electronics from the University of Leeds, England. Following an early career as a research scientist with a major multinational, Phil spent a few years in commercial and managerial roles within the high technology sector, later working full time as a software engineering consultant.

Operating as "The Mouse Whisperer" (http://www.mousewhisperer. co.uk), Phil has spent recent years involved solely in website and intranet design and development for an international portfolio of clients. Another of his websites, http://www.crackajax.net, is home to an active and fast-growing Ajax programming community.

Phil is currently based in southeast England. In his spare time, he still plays bass guitar in rock bands, despite being easily old enough to know better.

Dedication

To Sue, for her endless patience and support during the writing of this book—and at all other times, too.

Acknowledgments

I would like to offer my sincere thanks for the team at Sams Publishing, especially Linda Harrison, Shelley Johnston, Damon Jordan, Seth Kerney, Geneil Breeze, and Andrea Bledsoe.

Bill Bercik deserves special thanks, not only for his excellent work as technical editor, but also for his article at http://www.webpasties.com that inspired my interest in Ajax in the first place.

I would also like to express my gratitude to the countless individuals who have shared their knowledge and skill by writing open source software, Internet articles, and tutorials. Without their contributions, this book, and a great deal else, would not have been possible.

We Want to Hear from You!

As the reader of this book, *you* are our most important critic and commentator. We value your opinion and want to know what we're doing right, what we could do better, what areas you'd like to see us publish in, and any other words of wisdom you're willing to pass our way.

You can email or write me directly to let me know what you did or didn't like about this book—as well as what we can do to make our books stronger.

Please note that I cannot help you with technical problems related to the topic of this book, and that due to the high volume of mail I receive, I might not be able to reply to every message.

When you write, please be sure to include this book's title and author as well as your name and phone or email address. I will carefully review your comments and share them with the author and editors who worked on the book.

Email: webdev@samspublishing.com

Mail: Mark Taber
        Associate Publisher
        Sams Publishing
        800 East 96th Street
        Indianapolis, IN 46240 USA

Reader Services

Visit our website and register this book at www.samspublishing.com/register for convenient access to any updates, downloads, or errata that might be available for this book.

Introduction

Ajax is stirring up high levels of interest in the Internet development community. Ajax allows developers to provide visitors to their websites slick, intuitive user interfaces somewhat like those of desktop applications instead of using the traditional page-based web paradigm.

Based on well-known and understood technologies such as JavaScript and XML, Ajax is easily learned by those familiar with the mainstream web design technologies and does not require users to have any browser plugins or other special software.

About This Book

Part of the Sams Publishing *Teach Yourself in 10 Minutes* series, this book aims to teach the basics of building Ajax applications for the Internet. Divided into bite-sized lessons, each designed to take no more than about 10 minutes to complete, this volume offers

- A review of the technologies on which the World Wide Web is based

- Basic tutorials/refreshers in HTML, JavaScript, PHP, and XML

- An understanding of the architecture of Ajax applications

- Example Ajax coding projects

After completing all the lessons you'll be equipped to write and understand basic Ajax applications, including all necessary client- and server-side programming.

What Is Ajax?

Ajax stands for *Asynchronous Javascript And XML*. Although strictly speaking Ajax itself is not a technology, it mixes well-known programming techniques in an uncommon way to enable web developers to build

Internet applications with much more appealing user interfaces than those to which we have become accustomed.

When using popular desktop applications, we expect the results of our work to be made available immediately, without fuss, and without us having to wait for the whole screen to be redrawn by the program. While using a spreadsheet such as Excel, for instance, we expect the changes we make in one cell to propagate immediately through the neighboring cells while we continue to type, scroll the page, or use the mouse.

Unfortunately, this sort of interaction has seldom been available to users of web-based applications. Much more common is the experience of entering data into form fields, clicking on a button or link, and then sitting back while the page slowly reloads to exhibit the results of the request. In addition, we often find that the majority of the reloaded page consists of elements that are identical to those of the previous page and that have therefore been reloaded unnecessarily; background images, logos, and menus are frequent offenders.

Ajax promises us a solution to this problem. By working as an extra layer between the user's browser and the web server, Ajax handles server communications in the background, submitting server requests and processing the returned data. The results may then be integrated seamlessly into the page being viewed, without that page needing to be refreshed or a new one loaded.

In Ajax applications, such server requests are not necessarily synchronized with user actions such as clicking on buttons or links. A well-written Ajax application may already have asked of the server, and received, the data required by the user—perhaps before the user even knew she wanted it. This is the meaning of the *asynchronous* part of the Ajax acronym.

The parts of an Ajax application that happen "under the hood" of the user's browser, such as sending server queries and dealing with the returned data, are written in *JavaScript*, and *XML* is an increasingly popular means of coding and transferring formatted information used by Ajax to efficiently transfer data between server and client.

We'll look at all these techniques, and how they can be made to work together, as we work through the lessons.

Who This Book Is For

This volume is aimed primarily at web developers seeking to build better interfaces for the users of their web applications and programmers from desktop environments looking to transfer their applications to the Internet.

It also proves useful to web designers eager to learn how the latest techniques can offer new outlets for their creativity. Although the nature of Ajax applications means that they require some programming, all the required technologies are explained from first principles within the book, so even those with little or no programming experience should be able to follow the lessons without a great deal of difficulty.

What Do I Need To Use This Book?

The main requirement is to have an interest in exploring how people and computers might work better together. Although some programming experience, especially in JavaScript, will certainly be useful it is by no means mandatory because there are introductory tutorials in all the required technologies.

To try out the program code for yourself you need access to a web server and the means to upload files to it (for example, via File Transfer Protocol, usually called FTP). Make sure that your web host allows you to use PHP scripts on the server, though the majority do these days.

To write and edit program code you need a suitable text editor. Windows Notepad does the job perfectly well, though some specialized programmers' editors offer additional useful facilities such as line numbering and syntax highlighting. The appendix contains details of some excellent examples that may be downloaded and used free of charge.

Conventions Used in This Book

In addition to the main text of each lesson, you will find a number of boxes labeled as Tips, Notes, and Cautions.

Tip   Tips offer useful shortcuts or easier ways to achieve something.

Note   Notes are snippets of extra information relevant to the current theme of the text.

Caution   Cautions detail traps that may catch the unwary and advise how to avoid them.

Online Resources and Errata

Visit the Sams Publishing website at www.samspublishing.com where you can download the example code and obtain further information and details of errata.

LESSON 1
Anatomy of a Website

We have a lot of ground to cover in this book, so let's get to it. We'll begin by reviewing in this lesson what the World Wide Web is and where it came from. Afterward we'll take a look at some of the major components that make it work.

A Short History of the Web

In the late 1950s, the U.S. government formed the Advanced Research Projects Agency (ARPA). This was largely a response to the Russian success in launching the *Sputnik* satellite and employed some of the country's top scientific intellects in research work with U.S. military applications.

During the 1960s, the agency created a decentralized computer network known as ARPAnet. This embryonic network initially linked four computers located at the University of California at Los Angeles, Stanford Research Institute, the University of California at Santa Barbara, and the University of Utah, with more nodes added in the early 1970s.

The network had initially been designed using the then-new technology of packet switching and was intended as a communication system that would remain functional even if some nodes should be destroyed by a nuclear attack.

Email was implemented in 1972, closely followed by the telnet protocol for logging on to remote computers and the File Transfer Protocol (FTP), enabling file transfer between computers.

This developing network was enhanced further in subsequent years with improvements to many facets of its protocols and tools. However, it was not until 1989 when Tim Berners-Lee and his colleagues at the European particle physics laboratory CERN (*Conseil Européen pour le Recherche Nucléaire*) proposed the concept of linking documents with *hypertext* that the now familiar World Wide Web began to take shape. The year 1993 saw the introduction of Mosaic, the first graphical web browser and forerunner of the famous Netscape Navigator.

The use of hypertext pages and hyperlinks helped to define the page-based interface model that we still regard as the norm for web applications today.

Workings of the World Wide Web

The World Wide Web operates using a client/server networking principle. When you enter the URL (the web address) of a web page into your browser and click on Go, you ask the browser to make an *HTTP request* of the particular computer having that address. On receiving this request, that computer returns ("serves") the required page to you in a form that your browser can interpret and display. Figure 1.1 illustrates this relationship. In the case of the Internet, of course, the server and client computers may be located anywhere in the world.

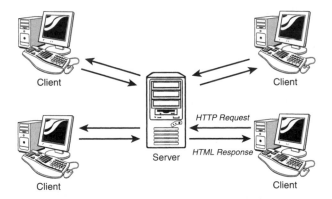

FIGURE 1.1 How web servers and clients (browsers) interact.

Lesson 3, "Sending Requests Using the HTTP Protocol," discusses the nitty-gritty of HTTP requests in more detail. For now, suffice to say that your HTTP request contains several pieces of information needed so that your page may be correctly identified and served to you, including the following:

- The domain at which the page is stored (for example, mydomain.com)

- The name of the page (This is the name of a file in the web server's file system—for example, mypage.html.)

- The names and values of any parameters that you want to send with your request

What Is a Web Page?

Anyone with some experience using the World Wide Web will be familiar with the term *web page*. The traditional user interface for websites involves the visitor navigating among a series of connected *pages* each containing text, images, and so forth, much like the pages of a magazine.

Generally, each web page is actually a separate file on the server. The collection of individual pages constituting a website is managed by a program called a *web server*.

Web Servers

A web server is a program that interprets HTTP requests and delivers the appropriate web page in a form that your browser can understand. Many examples are available, most running under either UNIX/Linux operating systems or under some version of Microsoft Windows.

 Caution   The term *web server* is often used in popular speech to refer to both the web server program—such as Apache—and the computer on which it runs.

Perhaps the best-known server application is the *Apache Web Server* from the Apache Software Foundation (http://www.apache.org), an open source project used to serve millions of websites around the world (see Figure 1.2).

FIGURE 1.2   The Apache Software Foundation home page at http://www.apache.org/ displayed in Internet Explorer.

Another example is Microsoft's IIS (Internet Information Services), often used on host computers running the Microsoft Windows operating system.

> **Note**   Not all Windows-based web hosts use IIS. Various other web servers are available for Windows, including a version of the popular Apache Web Server.

Server-Side Programming

Server-side programs, scripts, or languages, refer to programs that run on the server computer. Many languages and tools are available for server-side programming, including PHP, Java, and ASP (the latter being available only on servers running the Microsoft Windows operating system). Sophisticated server setups often also include databases of information that can be addressed by server-side scripts.

> **Note** Server-side programming in this book is carried out using the popular PHP scripting language, which is flexible, is easy to use, and can be run on nearly all servers. Ajax, however, can function equally well with any server-side scripting language.

The purposes of such scripts are many and various. In general, however, they all are designed to preprocess a web page before it is returned to you. By this we mean that some or all of the page content will have been modified to suit the context of your request—perhaps to display train times to a particular destination and on a specific date, or to show only those products from a catalog that match your stated hobbies and interests.

In this way server-side scripting allows web pages to be served with rich and varied content that would be beyond the scope of any design using only static pages—that is, pages with fixed content.

Web Browsers

A *web browser* is a program on a web surfer's computer that is used to interpret and display web pages. The first graphical web browser, Mosaic, eventually developed into the famous range of browsers produced by Netscape.

> **Note** By *graphical* web browser we mean one that can display not only the text elements of an HTML document but also images and colors. Typically, such browsers have a point-and-click interface using a mouse or similar pointing device.
>
> There also exist text-based web browsers, the best known of which is Lynx (http://lynx.browser.org/), which display HTML pages on character-based displays such as terminals, terminal emulators, and operating systems with command-line interfaces such as DOS.

The Netscape series of browsers, once the most successful available, were eventually joined by Microsoft's Internet Explorer offering, which subsequently went on to dominate the market.

Recent competitive efforts, though, have introduced a wide range of competing browser products including Opera, Safari, Konqueror, and especially Mozilla's Firefox, an open source web browser that has recently gained an enthusiastic following (see Figure 1.3).

Browsers are readily available for many computer operating systems, including the various versions of Microsoft Windows, UNIX/Linux, and Macintosh, as well as for other computing devices ranging from mobile telephones to PDAs (Personal Digital Assistants) and pocket computers.

FIGURE 1.3   The Firefox browser from Mozilla.org browsing the Firefox Project home page.

Client-Side Programming

We have already discussed how server scripts can improve your web experience by offering pages that contain rich and varied content created at the server and inserted into the page before it is sent to you.

Client-side programming, on the other hand, happens not at the server but right inside the user's browser *after* the page has been received. Such scripts allow you to carry out many tasks relating to the data in the received page, including performing calculations, changing display colors and styles, checking the validity of user input, and much more.

Nearly all browsers support some version or other of a client-side scripting language called JavaScript, which is an integral part of Ajax and is the language we'll be using in this book for client-side programming.

DNS—The Domain Name Service

Every computer connected to the Internet has a unique numerical address (called an *IP address*) assigned to it. However, when you want to view a particular website in your browser, you don't generally want to type in a series of numbers—you want to use the domain name of the site in question. After all, it's much easier to remember www.somedomain.com than something like 198.105.232.4.

When you request a web page by its domain name, your Internet service provider submits that domain name to a DNS server, which tries to look up the database entry associated with the name and obtain the corresponding IP address. If it's successful, you are connected to the site; otherwise, you receive an error.

The many DNS servers around the Internet are connected together into a network that constantly updates itself as changes are made. When DNS information for a website changes, the revised address information is propagated throughout the DNS servers of the entire Internet, typically within about 24 hours.

Summary

In Lesson 1 we discussed the history and development of the Internet and reviewed the functions of some of its major components including web servers and web browsers. We also considered the page-based nature of the traditional website user interface and had a brief look at what server- and client-side scripting can achieve to improve users' web surfing experience.

Lesson 2
Writing Web Pages in HTML

In this lesson we introduce HTML, the markup language behind virtually every page of the World Wide Web. A sound knowledge of HTML provides an excellent foundation for the Ajax applications discussed in later lessons.

Introducing HTML

It wouldn't be appropriate to try to give an exhaustive account of HTML (Hypertext Markup Language)—or, indeed, any of the other component technologies of Ajax—within this book. Instead we'll review the fundamental principles and give some code examples to illustrate them, paying particular attention to the subjects that will become relevant when we start to develop Ajax applications.

> **Tip** If you want to explore HTML in greater detail, Sams Publishing offers a number of titles that will help you, including *Sams Teach Yourself HTML 4 in 24 Hours* by Dick Oliver.

What Is HTML?

The World Wide Web is constructed from many millions of individual pages, and those pages are, in general, written in Hypertext Markup Language, better known as HTML.

That name gives away a lot of information about the nature of HTML. We use it to mark up our text documents so that web browsers know how to display them and to define hypertext links within them to provide navigation within or between them.

Anyone who (like me) can remember the old pre-WYSIWYG word processing programs will already be familiar with text markup. Most of these old applications required that special characters be placed at the beginning and end of sections of text that you wanted to be displayed as (for instance) bold, italic, or underlined text.

What Tools Are Needed to Write HTML?

Because the elements used in HTML markup employ only ordinary keyboard characters, all you really need is a good text editor to construct HTML pages. Many are available, and most operating systems have at least one such program already installed. If you're using some version of Windows, for example, the built-in Notepad application works just fine.

> **Tip**   Although Notepad is a perfectly serviceable text editor, many so-called *programmers' editors* are available offering useful additional functions such as line numbering and syntax highlighting. Many of these are under open source licences and can be downloaded and used at no cost. It is well worth considering using such an editor, especially for larger or more complex programming tasks.

> **Caution**   Although text editors are ideal for writing program code, the use of word processing software can cause problems due to unwanted markup and other symbols that such programs often embed in the output code. If you choose to use a word processor, make sure that it is capable of saving files as plain ASCII text.

Our First HTML Document

Let's jump right in and create a simple HTML document. Open Notepad (or whatever editor you've chosen to use) and enter the text shown in Listing 2.1. The HTML markup elements (often referred to as *tags*) are the character strings enclosed by < and >.

LISTING 2.1   testpage.html

```
<!DOCTYPE HTML PUBLIC "-//W3C//DTD HTML 4.01 Transitional//EN"
➥"http://www.w3.org/TR/html4/loose.dtd">
<html>
<head>
<title>A Simple HTML Document</title>
</head>
<body>
<h1>My HTML Page</h1>
Welcome to my first page written in HTML.<br />
This is simply a text document with HTML markup to show some
words in <b>bold</b> and some other words in <i>italics</i>.
<br />
</body>
</html>
```

Now save the document somewhere on your computer, giving it the name testpage.html.

If you now load that page into your favorite browser, such as Internet Explorer or Firefox, you should see something like the window displayed in Figure 2.1.

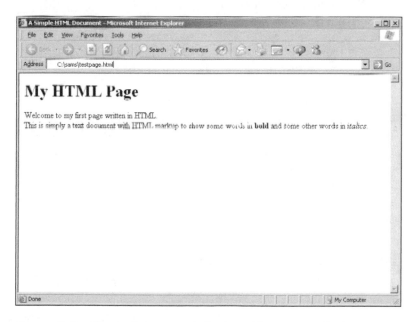

FIGURE 2.1   Our test document displayed in Internet Explorer.

Elements of an HTML Page

Let's look at Listing 2.1 in a little more detail.

The first element on the page is known as the DOCTYPE element. Its purpose is to notify the browser of the "flavor" of HTML used in the document. The DOCTYPE element used throughout this book refers to *HTML 4.0 Transitional*, a fairly forgiving version of the HTML specification that allows the use of some earlier markup styles and structures in addition to the latest HTML 4.0 specifications.

The DOCTYPE element must always occur right at the beginning of the HTML document.

Next, note that the remainder of the document is enclosed by the elements <html> at the start of the page and </html> at the end. These tags notify the browser that what lies between should be interpreted and displayed as an HTML document.

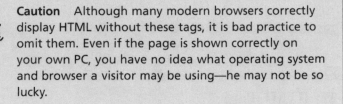

Caution Although many modern browsers correctly display HTML without these tags, it is bad practice to omit them. Even if the page is shown correctly on your own PC, you have no idea what operating system and browser a visitor may be using—he may not be so lucky.

The document within these outer tags is split into two further sections. The first is enclosed in <head> and </head> tags, and the second is contained between <body> and </body>. Essentially, the document's head section is used to store information about the document that is not to be displayed in the browser window, whereas the body of the document contains text to be interpreted and displayed to the user via the browser window.

The <head> of the Document

From Listing 2.1 we can see that the head section of our simple HTML document contains only one line—the words A Simple HTML Document enclosed in <title> and </title> tags.

Remember that the head section contains information that is not to be displayed in the browser window. This is not, then, the title displayed at the top of our page text, as you can confirm by looking again at Figure 2.1. Neither does the document title refer to the filename of the document, which in this case is testpage.html.

In fact, the document title fulfils a number of functions, among them:

- Search engines often use the page title (among other factors) to help them decide what a page is about.

- When you bookmark a page, it is generally saved by default as the document title.

- Most browsers, when minimized, display the title of the current document on their icon or taskbar button.

It's important, therefore, to choose a meaningful and descriptive title for each page that you create.

Many other element types are used in the head section of a document, including link, meta, and script elements. Although we don't give an account of them here, they are described throughout the book as they occur.

The Document <body>

Referring again to Listing 2.1, we can clearly see that the content of the document's body section is made up of the text we want to display on the page, plus some tags that help us to define how that text should look.

To define that certain words should appear in bold type, for example, we enclose those words in <b> and </b> tags. Similarly, to convert certain words into an italic typeface, we can use the <i> and </i> tags.

The heading, My HTML Page, is enclosed between <h1> and </h1> tags. These indicate that we intend the enclosed text to be a heading. HTML allows for six levels of headings, from h1 (the most prominent) to h6. You can use any of the intermediate values h2, h3, h4, and h5 to display pages having various levels of subtitles, for instance corresponding to chapter, section, and paragraph headings. Anything displayed within header tags is displayed on a line by itself.

All the tags discussed so far have been *containers*—that is, they consist of opening and closing tags between which you place the text that you want these tags to act upon. Some elements, however, are not containers but can be used alone. Listing 2.1 shows one such element: the <br /> tag, which signifies a line break. Another example is <hr /> (a horizontal line).

> **Tip**   If you want to write in the body section of the HTML page but *don't* want it to be interpreted by the browser and therefore displayed on the screen, you may do so by writing it as a *comment*. HTML comments start with the character string <!-- and end with the string --> as in this example:
>
> ```
> <!-- this is just a comment and won't be displayed
> in the browser -->
> ```

Adding Attributes to HTML Elements

Occasionally there is a need to specify exactly how a markup tag should behave. In such cases you can add (usually within the opening tag) parameter and value pairs, known as *attributes*, to change the behavior of the element:

```
<body bgcolor="#cccccc">
… page content goes here …
</body>
```

In this example, the behavior of the <body> tag has been modified by adjusting its BGCOLOR (background color) property to a light gray. Figure 2.2 shows the effect this has if applied to our file testpage.html:

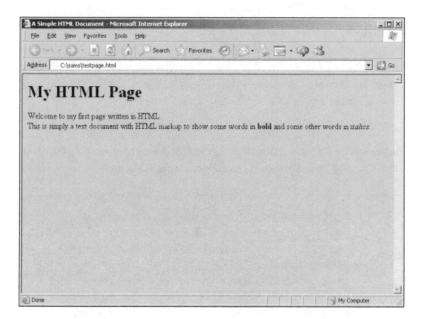

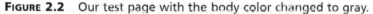

FIGURE 2.2   Our test page with the body color changed to gray.

> **Tip**   Color values in HTML are coded using a hexadecimal system. Each color value is made up from three component values, corresponding to red, green, and blue. Each of the color values can range from hex 00 to hex ff (zero to 255 in decimal notation). The three hex numbers are concatenated into a string prefixed with a hash character #. The color value #000000 therefore corresponds to black, and #ffffff to pure white.

Images

Images can be inserted in our page by means of the <img /> tag. In this case we specify the source file of the image as a parameter by using the src attribute. Other aspects of the image display that we can alter this way include the borders, width, and height of the image:

```
<img src="myimagefile.jpg" border="2" width="250" height="175" />
```

Border width, image width, and image height are in numbers of *pixels* (the "dots" formed by individual picture elements on the screen).

> **Tip**   A further useful attribute for images is alt, which is an abbreviation of *alternative text*. This specifies a short description of the image that will be offered to users whose browsers cannot, or are configured not to, display images. Alternative text can also be important in making your website accessible to those with visual impairment and other disabilities:
>
> ```
> <img src="myimagefile.jpg" alt="Description of Image"
> ➥/>
> ```

Tables

Often you want to display information in tabular format, and HTML has a set of elements designed specifically for this purpose:

```
<table>
<tr><th>Column Header 1</th><th>Column Header 2</th></tr>
<tr><td>Data Cell 1</td><td>Data Cell 2</td></tr>
<tr><td>Data Cell 3</td><td>Data Cell 4</td></tr>
</table>
```

The <table> and </table> tags contain a nested hierarchy of other tags, including <tr> and </tr>, which define individual table rows; <th> and </th>, which indicate cells in the table's header; and <td> and </td>, which contain individual cells of table data.

Look ahead to Figure 2.3 to see an example of how a table looks when displayed in a browser window.

Hyperlinks

Hypertext links (*hyperlinks*) are fundamental to the operation of HTML. By clicking on a hyperlink, you can navigate to a new location, be that to another point on the current page or to some point on a different page on another website entirely.

Links are contained within an <a>, or anchor tag, a container tag that encloses the content that will become the link. The destination of the link is passed to this tag as a parameter href:

```
Here is <a href="newpage.html">my hyperlink</a>
```

Clicking on the words my hyperlink in the above example results in the browser requesting the page newpage.html.

> **Tip** A hyperlink can contain images as well as, or instead of, text. Look at this example:
>
> ```
> <a href="newpage.html"><img src="picfile.gif" /></a>
> ```
>
> Here, a user can click on the image picfile.gif to navigate to newpage.html.

A More Advanced HTML Page

Let's revisit our testpage.html and add some extra elements. Listing ? ? shows seville.html, developed from our original HTML page but with different content in the <body> section of the document. Figure 2.3 shows how the page looks when displayed, this time in Mozilla Firefox.

Now we have applied a background tint to the body area of the document. The content of the body area has been centered on the page, and that content now includes an image (which we've given a two-pixel-wide border), a heading and a subheading, a simple table, and some text.

LISTING 2.2 seville.html

```
<!DOCTYPE HTML PUBLIC "-//W3C//DTD HTML 4.01
➥Transitional//EN" "http://www.w3.org/TR/html4/loose.dtd">
```

continues

LISTING 2.2   Continued

```html
<html>
<head>
<title>A Simple HTML Document</title>
</head>
<body bgcolor="#cccccc">
<center>
<img src="cathedral.jpg" border="2" alt="Cathedral" />
<h1>Guide to Seville</h1>
<h3>A brief guide to the attractions</h3>
<table border="2">
<tr>
  <th bgcolor="#aaaaaa">Attraction</th>
  <th bgcolor="#aaaaaa">Description</th>
</tr>
<tr>
  <td>Cathedral</td>
  <td>Dating back to the 15th century</td>
</tr>
<tr>
  <td>Alcazar</td>
  <td>The medieval Islamic palace</td>
</tr>
</table>
<p>Enjoy your stay in beautiful Seville.</p>
</center>
</body>
</html>
```

Let's take a closer look at some of the code.

First, we used the BGCOLOR property of the <body> tag to provide the overall background tint for the page:

```html
<body bgcolor="#cccccc">
```

Everything in the body area is contained between the <center> tag (immediately after the body tag) and its partner </center>, immediately before the closing body tag. This ensures that all of our content is centered on the page.

The main heading is enclosed in <h1> … </h1> tags as previously, but is now followed by a subheading using <h3> … </h3> tags to provide a slightly smaller font size.

By using the border property in our opening <table> tag, we set a border width of two pixels for the table:

```
<table border="2">
```

Meanwhile we darkened the background of the table's header cells slightly by using the BGCOLOR property of the <th> elements:

```
<th bgcolor="#aaaaaa">Attraction</th>
```

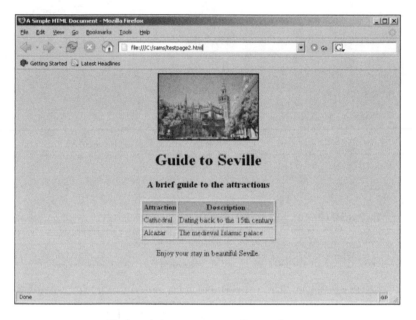

FIGURE 2.3   seville.html shown in Mozilla Firefox.

Some Useful HTML Tags

Table 2.1 lists some of the more popular HTML tags.

TABLE 2.1   Some Common HTML Markup Elements

Document Tags

<html>..</html>	The entire document
<head>..</head>	Document head

continues

TABLE 2.1 Continued

Document Tags

`<body>..</body>`	Document body
`<title>..</title>`	Document title

Style Tags

`<a>..</a>`	Hyperlink
`<b>..</b>`	Bold text
`<em>..</em>`	Emphasized text
`<font>..</font>`	Changed font
`<i>..</i>`	Italic text
`<small>..</small>`	Small text
`<table>..</table>`	Table
`<tr>..</tr>`	Table row
`<th>..</th>`	Cell in table header
`<td>..</td>`	Cell in table body
`<ul>..</ul>`	Bulleted list
`<ol>..</ol>`	Ordered (numbered) list
`<li>..</li>`	List item in bulleted or ordered list

Tip The World Wide Web Consortium is responsible for administering the definitions of HTML, HTTP, XML, and many other web technologies. Its website is at http://www.w3.org/.

Cascading Style Sheets in Two Minutes

The preceding approach to styling web pages has a few downsides.

First, you need to explicitly state the attributes of each page element. When you want to change the look of the page, you need to go through the source code line by line and change every instance of every attribute. This may be okay with a few simple pages, but as the amount of content increases, the pages become more difficult to maintain. Additionally, the attributes applied to HTML elements allow only limited scope for you to adjust how they are displayed.

Wouldn't it be better to make one change to the code and have that change applied to all HTML elements of a given type? As I'm sure you've already guessed, you can.

To achieve this goal you use *styles*. Styles may be embedded within your HTML document by using style tags in the head of the document:

```
<style type="text/css">
  ... style definition statements ...
</style>
```

Alternatively, they may be linked from an external file, using a link element, once again placed in the head section of the document:

```
<link rel=stylesheet href="mystylesheet.css" type="text/css" />
```

> **Tip** You can even define styles on-the-fly. These are known as *inline styles* and can be applied to individual HTML elements. Taking the body tag of Listing 2.2 as an example:
>
> ```
> <body bgcolor="#cccccc">
> ```
>
> You could achieve the same effect using an inline style:
>
> ```
> <body style="background-color:#cccccc">
> ```

Setting Style Sheet Rules

Style sheets allow you to set styling rules for the various HTML elements. A rule has two components: the selector, which identifies which HTML tag the rule should affect, and the declaration, which contains your styling rule. The following example defines a style for the paragraph element, <p>:

```
P {color: #333333}
```

This example determines that any text enclosed in paragraph tags <p> … </p> should be displayed using dark gray text. You may also specify more than one rule for each tag. Suppose that, in addition to gray text, you want all text in the paragraph element to be displayed in italics:

```
P {color: #333333; font-style: italic}
```

A style sheet can contain as many such rules as you require.

You may also apply a declaration to more than one tag at once, by separating the tag selectors with commas. The following rule determines that all h1, h2, and h3 headings appear in blue text:

```
H1, H2, H3 {color: blue}
```

Summary

This lesson discussed the basics of web page layout using Hypertext Markup Language, including the structure of HTML documents, examples of HTML page elements, and page styling using both element attributes and cascading style sheets.

LESSON 3

Sending Requests Using HTTP

Various protocols are used for communication over the World Wide Web, perhaps the most important being HTTP, the protocol that is also fundamental to Ajax applications. This lesson introduces the HTTP protocol and shows how it is used to request and receive information.

Introducing HTTP

HTTP or *Hypertext Transfer Protocol* is the main protocol of the World Wide Web. When you request a web page by typing its address into your web browser, that request is sent using HTTP. The browser is an *HTTP client*, and the web page server is (unsurprisingly) an *HTTP server*.

In essence, HTTP defines a set of rules regarding how messages and other data should be formatted and exchanged between servers and browsers.

Why Do I Need To Know About This?

Ajax sends server requests using the HTTP protocol. It's important to recognize the different types of HTTP requests and the responses that the server may return. Ajax applications need to construct HTTP requests to query the server and will base decisions about what to do next on the content of HTTP responses from the server.

What Is (and Isn't) Covered in This Lesson

It would be possible to fill the whole book with information on the HTTP protocol, but here we simply discuss it in terms of its roles in requesting web pages and passing information between them.

In this lesson you'll look at the construction of HTTP requests and responses and see how HTML forms use such requests to transfer data between web pages.

 Tip   For a detailed account of HTTP, see Sams Publishing's *HTTP Developer's Handbook* by Chris Shiflett.

The HTTP Request and Response

The HTTP protocol can be likened to a conversation based on a series of questions and answers, which we refer to respectively as *HTTP requests* and *HTTP responses*.

The contents of HTTP requests and responses are easy to read and understand, being near to plain English in their syntax.

This section examines the structure of these requests and responses, along with a few examples of the sorts of data they may contain.

The HTTP Request

After opening a connection to the intended server, the HTTP client transmits a request in the following format:

- An opening line

- Optionally, a number of *header lines*

- A blank line

- Optionally, a message body

The opening line is generally split into three parts; the name of the *method*, the path to the required *server resource*, and the *HTTP version* being used. A typical opening line might read:

```
GET /sams/testpage.html HTTP/1.0
```

In this line we are telling the server that we are sending an HTTP request of type GET (explained more fully in the next section), we are sending this using HTTP version 1.0, and the server resource we require (including its local path) is

`/sams/testpage.html.`

> **Note** In this example the server resource we seek is on our own server, so we have quoted a relative path. It could of course be on another server elsewhere, in which case the server resource would include the full URL.

Header lines are used to send information about the request, or about the data being sent in the message body. One parameter and value pair is sent per line, the parameter and value being separated by a colon. Here's an example:

`User-Agent: [name of program sending request]`

For instance, Internet Explorer v5.5 offers something like the following:

`User-agent: Mozilla/4.0 (compatible; MSIE 5.5; Windows NT 5.0)`

A further example of a common request header is the `Accept:` header, which states what sort(s) of information will be found acceptable as a response from the server:

`Accept: text/plain, text/html`

By issuing the header in the preceding example, the request is informing the server that the sending application can accept either plain text or HTML responses (that is, it is not equipped to deal with, say, an audio or video file) .

> **Note** HTTP request methods include POST, GET, PUT, DELETE, and HEAD. By far the most interesting in our pursuit of Ajax are the GET and POST requests. The PUT, DELETE, and HEAD requests are not covered here.

The HTTP Response

In answer to such a request, the server typically issues an HTTP response, the first line of which is often referred to as the *status line*. In that line the server echoes the HTTP version and gives a response status code (which is a three-digit integer) and a short message known as a *reason phrase*. Here's an example HTTP response:

```
HTTP/1.0 200 OK
```

The response status code and reason phrase are essentially intended as machine-and human-readable versions of the same message, though the reason phrase may actually vary a little from server to server. Table 3.1 lists some examples of common status codes and reason phrases. The first digit of the status code usually gives some clue about the nature of the message:

- 1**—Information
- 2**—Success
- 3**—Redirected
- 4**—Client error
- 5**—Server error

TABLE 3.1   Some Commonly Encountered HTTP Response Status Codes

Status Code	Explanation
200 - OK	The request succeeded.
204 - No Content	The document contains no data.
301 - Moved Permanently	The resource has permanently moved to a different URI.
401 - Not Authorized	The request needs user authentication.
403 - Forbidden	The server has refused to fulfill the request.
404 - Not Found	The requested resource does not exist on the server.

Status Code	Explanation
408 - Request Timeout	The client failed to send a request in the time allowed by the server.
500 - Server Error	Due to a malfunctioning script, server configuration error or similar.

> **Tip**   A detailed list of status codes is maintained by the World Wide Web Consortium, W3C, and is available at http://www.w3.org/Protocols/rfc2616/rfc2616-sec10.html.

The response may also contain header lines each containing a header and value pair similar to those of the HTTP request but generally containing information about the server and/or the resource being returned:

```
Server: Apache/1.3.22
Last-Modified: Fri, 24 Dec 1999 13:33:59 GMT
```

HTML Forms

Web pages often contain fields where you can enter information. Examples include select boxes, check boxes, and fields where you can type information. Table 3.2 lists some popular HTML form tags.

TABLE 3.2   Some Common HTML Form Tags

Tag	Description
<form>...</form>	Container for the entire form
<input />	Data entry element; includes text, password, check box and radio button fields, and submit and reset buttons
<select>...</select>	Drop-down select box
<option>...</option>	Selectable option within select box
<textarea>...</textarea>	Text entry field with multiple rows

After you have completed the form you are usually invited to submit it, using an appropriately labeled button or other page element.

At this point, the HTML form constructs and sends an HTTP request from the user-entered data. The form can use either the GET or POST request type, as specified in the method attribute of the <form> tag.

GET and POST Requests

Occasionally you may hear it said that the difference between GET and POST requests is that GET requests are just for GETting (that is, retrieving) data, whereas POST requests can have many uses, such as uploading data, sending mail, and so on.

Although there may be some merit in this rule of thumb, it's instructive to consider the differences between these two HTTP requests in terms of how they are constructed.

A GET request encodes the message it sends into a *query string*, which is appended to the URL of the server resource. A POST request, on the other hand, sends its message in the *message body* of the request. What actually happens at this point is that the entered data is encoded and sent, via an HTTP request, to the URL declared in the action attribute of the form, where the submitted data will be processed in some way.

Whether the HTTP request is of type GET or POST and the URL to which the form is sent are both determined in the HTML markup of the form. Let's look at the HTML code of a typical form:

```
<form action="http://www.sometargetdomain.com/somepage.htm"
➥    method="post">
Your Surname: <input type="text" size="50" name="surname" />
<br />
<input type="submit" value="Send" />
</form>
```

This snippet of code, when embedded in a web page, produces the simple form shown in Figure 3.1.

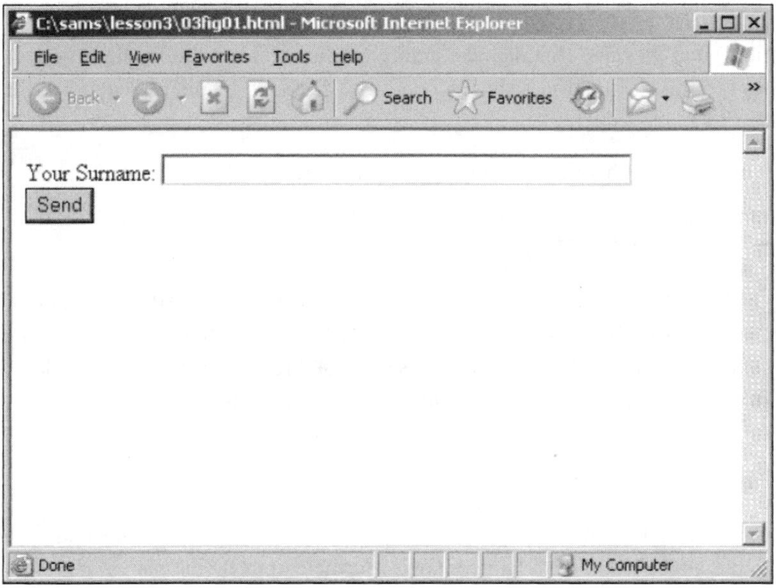

FIGURE 3.1 A simple HTML form.

Let's take a look at the code, line by line. First, we begin the form by using the `<form>` tag, and in this example we give the tag two attributes. The `action` attribute determines the URL to which the submitted form will be sent. This may be to another page on the same server and described by a relative path, or to a remote domain, as in the code behind the form in Figure 3.1.

Next we find the attribute method, which determines whether we want the data to be submitted with a GET or a POST request.

Now suppose that we completed the form by entering the value *Ballard* into the surname field. On submitting the form by clicking the Send button, we are taken to http://www.sometargetdomain.com/somepage.htm, where the submitted data will be processed—perhaps adding the surname to a database, for example.

The variable `surname` (the `name` attribute given to the `Your Surname` input field) and its value (the data we entered in that field) will also have been sent to this destination page, encoded into the body of the `POST` request and invisible to users.

Now suppose that the first line of the form code reads as follows:

```
<form action="http://www.sometargetdomain.com/somepage.htm"
➥       method="get">
```

On using the form, we would still be taken to the same destination, and the same variable and its value would also be transmitted. This time, however, the form would construct and send a `GET` request containing the data from the form. Looking at the address bar of the browser, after successfully submitting the form, we would find that it now contains:

```
http://www.example.com/page.htm?surname=Ballard
```

Here we can see how the parameter and its value have been appended to the URL. If the form had contained further input fields, the values entered in those fields would also have been appended to the URL as *parameter=value* pairs, with each pair separated by an & character. Here's an example in which we assume that the form has a further text input field called `firstname`:

```
http://www.example.com/page.htm?surname=Ballard&firstname=Phil
```

Some characters, such as spaces and various punctuation marks, are not allowed to be transmitted in their original form. The HTML form encodes these characters into a form that can be transmitted correctly. An equivalent process decodes these values at the receiving page before processing them, thus making the encoding/decoding operation essentially invisible to the user. We can, however, see what this encoding looks like by making a `GET` request and examining the URL constructed in doing so.

Suppose that instead of the `surname` field in our form we have a `fullname` field that asks for the full name of the user and encodes that information into a `GET` request. Then, after submitting the form, we might see the following URL in the browser:

```
http://www.example.com/page.htm?fullname=Phil+Ballard
```

Here the space in the name has been replaced by the + character; the decoding process at the receiving end removes this character and replaces the space.

> **Note** In many cases, you may use either the POST or GET method for your form submissions and achieve essentially identical results. The difference becomes important, however, when you learn how to construct server calls in Ajax applications.

The XMLHTTPRequest object at the heart of all Ajax applications uses HTTP to make requests of the server and receive responses. The content of these HTTP requests are essentially identical to those generated when an HTML form is submitted.

Summary

This lesson covered some basics of server requests and responses using the HTTP protocol, the main communications protocol of the World Wide Web. In particular, we discussed how GET and POST requests are constructed, and how they are used in HTML forms. Additionally, we saw some examples of responses to these requests that we might receive from the server.

LESSON 4

Client-Side Coding Using JavaScript

In this lesson we introduce the concept of client-side scripting using JavaScript. Client-side scripts are embedded in web pages and executed by a JavaScript interpreter built into the browser. They add extra functionality to an otherwise static HTML page.

About JavaScript

JavaScript was developed from a language called LiveScript, which was developed by Netscape for use in its early browsers. JavaScript source code is embedded within the HTML code of web pages and interpreted and executed by the browser when the page is displayed.

Using JavaScript, you can add extra functionality to your web pages. Examples include

- Change the way page elements are displayed

- Add animation and other image effects

- Open pop-up windows and dialogs

- Check the validity of user-entered data

Nearly all modern browsers support JavaScript, though with a few differences in some commands. Where these occur, they are described in the text.

> **Caution** Although JavaScript is likely to be supported by your browser, it is usually possible for the browser options to be configured so as to disable its use. If you find that you cannot get any JavaScript commands to work, consult your browser's help files to find out how to check whether JavaScript is correctly enabled.

> **Note** Microsoft's Internet Explorer browser actually runs a proprietary Microsoft language called Jscript, instead of JavaScript. The two are, however, virtually identical and therefore largely compatible. Where differences occur, they are described in the text.

Why Do I Need To Know About JavaScript?

The *j* in Ajax stands for JavaScript; you use functions written in this language and embedded within your web pages to formulate Ajax server calls and to handle and process the response returned from the server.

What Is (and Isn't) Covered in This Lesson

There is no room here for an exhaustive guide to all JavaScript's functions. Instead this lesson concentrates on those aspects of the language necessary for later developing Ajax applications.

After completing this lesson, you'll have experience with the following:

- Embedding JavaScript commands and external JavaScript files into web pages

- Using some of the common JavaScript commands

- Using event handlers to launch JavaScript commands

- Working with JavaScript variables and objects

- Abstracting JavaScript commands into functions

> 💡 **Tip** For a much more thorough course in JavaScript, try *Sams Teach Yourself JavaScript in 24 Hours* by Michael Moncur.

JavaScript Basics

JavaScript commands can be embedded directly into HTML pages by placing them between <script> ...</script> tags. It is also common for JavaScript functions to be kept in a separate file on the server (usually with a file extension .js) and linked to HTML files where required, by placing a line like this into the head of the HTML file:

```
<SCRIPT language="JavaScript" SRC="myJS.js"></SCRIPT>
```

This allows you to call any JavaScript within the file myJS.js, just as if that source code had been typed directly into your own web page.

> 💡 **Tip** Placing JavaScript functions into external files allows them to be made available to a number of different web pages without having to retype any code. It also makes them easier to maintain because the latest version is automatically linked into the calling HTML page each time that page is requested.
>
> It is possible to build up substantial JavaScript libraries in this way, linking them into web pages when their particular functions are required.

In at the Deep End

Let's get right to it and add a JavaScript command to the simple web page we developed in Lesson 2, "Writing Web Pages in HTML."

Open your favorite text editor and load up seville.html (Listing 2.2 from Lesson 2). We're going to add the following code to the page, immediately after the </p> (the closing paragraph tag) on line 24:

```
<script language="JavaScript" type="text/javascript">
document.writeln("This line was written using JavaScript!");
</script>
```

 Caution JavaScript, unlike HTML, is case sensitive. When entering JavaScript commands, be careful not to enter characters in the incorrect case, or errors will occur.

The whole of the source code with the extra lines added is shown in Listing 4.1. Make sure that you have added the code correctly; then save the file as testpage3.html and load it into your favorite browser.

LISTING 4.1 Adding JavaScript to an HTML Page

```
<!DOCTYPE HTML PUBLIC "-//W3C//DTD HTML 4.01
➥Transitional//EN" "http://www.w3.org/TR/html4/
➥loose.dtd">
<html>
<head>
<title>A Simple HTML Document</title>
</head>
<body bgcolor="#cccccc">
<center>
<img src="cathedral.jpg" border="2" alt="Cathedral" />
<h1>A More Advanced HTML Page</h1>
<h3>Welcome to my second page written in HTML.</h3>
<table border="2">
<tr>
  <th bgcolor="#aaaaaa">Vegetables</th>
  <th bgcolor="#aaaaaa">Fruits</th>
</tr>
<tr>
  <td>Carrot</td>
  <td>Apple</td>
</tr>
<tr>
  <td>Cabbage</td>
  <td>Orange</td>
</tr>
</table><br />
```

continues

LISTING 4.1 Continued

```
<p>... and here's some text in a paragraph.</p>
<script language="JavaScript" type="text/javascript">
document.writeln("This line was written using JavaScript!")
</script>
</center>
</body>
</html>
```

If all has gone well, the page should now be like that shown in Figure 4.1. You should now be able to see an extra line of text toward the bottom of the page saying "This line was written using JavaScript!"

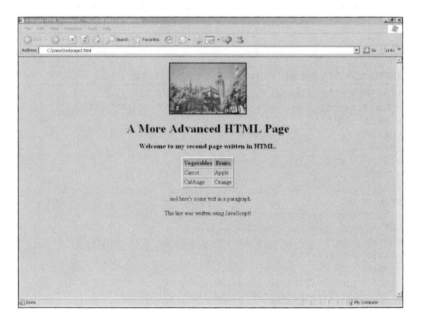

FIGURE 4.1   HTML document including one line written by JavaScript.

Let's look at our JavaScript code. The first item is the `<script>` tag, and here we have included the definition

```
Language="JavaScript"
```

which tells the browser that the statements contained within this script element should be interpreted as JavaScript.

Also in this tag appears the attribute

```
type="text/javascript"
```

This declares that the script enclosed in the element is written in JavaScript.

>
> **Tip** There are other possible languages in which such scripts could be written; each has its own type declaration such as
>
> ```
> type="text/vbscript"
> ```
>
> or
>
> ```
> type="text/xml"
> ```

The script is ended on the next to the last line with the familiar `</script>` tag.

Now for the meat in the sandwich:

```
document.writeln("This line was written using JavaScript!")
```

JavaScript (in common with many other programming languages) uses the concept of objects. The word document in this line of code refers to the object on which we want our JavaScript command to operate. In this case, we are dealing with the document object, which is the entire HTML document (including any embedded JavaScript code) that we are displaying in the browser. We'll have a further look at objects later in the lesson.

The term `writeln` describes the operation we want JavaScript to perform on the document object. We say it is a *method* of the document object, in this case one that writes a line of text into the document.

> **Note** In addition to methods, objects also possess *properties*. Such properties tell you something about the object, as opposed to the object's methods, which perform actions upon it.

The string within the parentheses we refer to as the *argument* that we pass to the `writeln` method. In this case it tells the method what to write to the document object.

Including JavaScript in HTML Pages

We can include as many `<script>...</script>` tags in our page as we need. However, we must pay some attention to where in the document they are placed.

JavaScript commands are executed in the order in which they appear in the page. Note from Listing 4.1 that we entered our JavaScript code at exactly the place in the document where we want the new text to appear.

JavaScript can also be added to the head section of the HTML page. This is a popular place to keep JavaScript functions, which we'll describe shortly.

Event Handlers

Often you want your JavaScript code to be executed because something specific has occurred. In an HTML form, for instance, you may decide to have JavaScript check the validity of the data entered by the user at the moment when the form is submitted. On another occasion, you may want to alert your user by opening a warning dialog whenever a particular button is clicked.

To achieve these effects you use special interfaces provided by the browser and known as *event handlers*. Event handlers allow you to call JavaScript methods automatically when certain types of events occur. Consider the following code:

```
<form>
<input type="button" value="Click Here"
➥     onClick="alert('Thanks for clicking!')">
</form>
```

Here we capture the action of the user clicking the button, using the `onClick` event handler. When the user's click is detected, the script carries out the instructions listed in the `onClick` attribute of the `input` tag:

```
onClick="alert('Thanks for clicking!')"
```

This line calls the JavaScript `alert` method, which pops up a dialog box displaying a message and an OK button. The message to be displayed in the alert dialog is contained in the string passed to the alert method as an argument.

Let's add this code to our HTML document, as shown in Listing 4.2. Save the page as testpage4.html after you've made the changes and load it into the browser.

LISTING 4.2   Calling `alert()` from the `onClick` Event Handler

```
<!DOCTYPE HTML PUBLIC "-//W3C//DTD HTML 4.01 Transitional
➥//EN" "http://www.w3.org/TR/html4/loose.dtd">
<html>
<head>
<title>A Simple HTML Document</title>
</head>
<body bgcolor="#cccccc">
<center>
<img src="cathedral.jpg" border="2" alt="Cathedral" />
<h1>A More Advanced HTML Page</h1>
<h3>Welcome to my second page written in HTML.</h3>
<table border="2">
<tr>
   <th bgcolor="#aaaaaa">Vegetables</th>
   <th bgcolor="#aaaaaa">Fruits</th>
</tr>
<tr>
   <td>Carrot</td>
   <td>Apple</td>
</tr>
<tr>
   <td>Cabbage</td>
   <td>Orange</td>
</tr>
</table><br />
<p>... and here's some text in a paragraph.</p>
<script language="JavaScript" type="text/javascript">
document.writeln("This line was written using JavaScript!")
</script>
<form>
<input type="button" value="Click Here" onClick="alert
➥('Thanks for clicking!')">
</form>
</center>
</body>
</html>
```

Our HTML page should now show our new button, as in Figure 4.2.

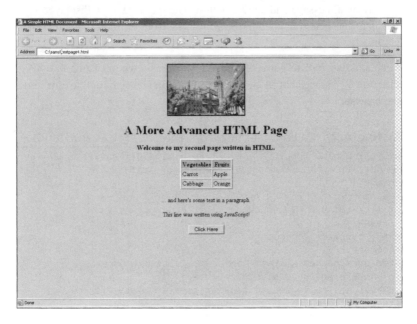

FIGURE 4.2   The new Click Here button in our web page.

Go ahead and click on the button. If everything goes according to plan, an alert dialog pops open as shown in Figure 4.3. You can click OK to clear the dialog.

Creating Functions

Often you will need to combine various JavaScript methods and objects, perhaps using many lines of code. JavaScript allows you to compose such blocks of instructions and name them, making your code easier to write, understand, and maintain.

For example, let's use another event handler, but this time we'll use it to call a function rather than to directly call a JavaScript method.

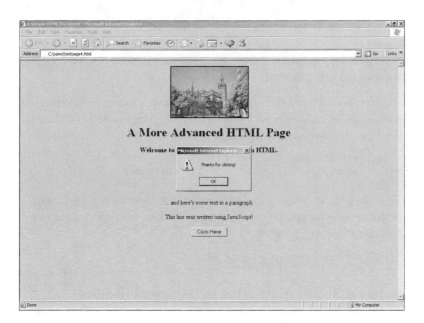

FIGURE 4.3   The dialog that appears after you click on the new button.

Here's the code for our function, which we'll place in the head section of our HTML document:

```
<script language="JavaScript">
function showAlert()
{
  alert("A Picture of Seville")
}
</script>
```

> **Note**   Note that a function definition always starts with the word `function` followed by the function's name. The statements within a function are contained within curly braces {}.

Within the usual `<script>` tags, we have now defined a function called `showAlert`, which carries out the commands contained within the curly braces. In this case, there is only one command, a call to the previously encountered `alert` method.

We want this alert dialog to appear when the user's mouse passes over the photograph in our web page. We are therefore going to add an attribute to the `<img>` tag that contains the image, as follows:

```
<img src="cathedral.jpg" border="2"
➥    onMouseOver="showAlert()" alt="Cathedral" />
```

This line uses the `onMouseOver` event handler to detect when the cursor enters the area occupied by the photograph. When this happens, our new function `showAlert` is called.

Listing 4.3 shows the revised code.

LISTING 4.3   Using the `onMouseOver` Event Handler

```
<!DOCTYPE HTML PUBLIC "-//W3C//DTD HTML 4.01 Transitional//EN"
"http://www.w3.org/TR/html4/loose.dtd">
<html>
<head>
<title>A Simple HTML Document</title>
<script language="JavaScript" type="text/javascript">
function showAlert()
{
alert("A Picture of Seville")
}
</script>
</head>
<body bgcolor="#cccccc">
<center>
<img src="cathedral.jpg" border="2" alt="Cathedral"
➥onMouseOver="showAlert()" />
<h1>A More Advanced HTML Page</h1>
<h3>Welcome to my second page written in HTML.</h3>
<table border="2">
<tr>
   <th bgcolor="#aaaaaa">Vegetables</th>
   <th bgcolor="#aaaaaa">Fruits</th>
</tr>
<tr>
   <td>Carrot</td>
```

```
  <td>Apple</td>
</tr>
<tr>
  <td>Cabbage</td>
  <td>Orange</td>
</tr>
</table><br />
<p>... and here's some text in a paragraph.</p>
<script language="JavaScript" type="text/javascript">
document.writeln("This line was written using JavaScript!")
</script>
<form>
<input type="button" value="Click Here" onClick="alert
➥('Thanks for clicking!')">
</form>
</center>
</body>
</html>
```

With this HTML document loaded into your browser, roll your mouse
over the photograph. An alert box should appear with the message "A
Picture of Seville".

Passing Arguments to Functions

Of course, we could easily call our function from a wide variety of event
handlers within our page and have it pop open an alert dialog.
Unfortunately, the alert would always contain the message "A Picture of
Seville", which is not very useful!

Wouldn't it be good if we could tell the function what message to display so
that we could have different alert messages for different circumstances? We
can achieve this by passing the message to our function as an argument:

```
<script language="JavaScript" type="text/javascript">
function showAlert(message)
{
  alert(message)
}
</script>
```

The function now "expects" to find the text for the message defined
passed as an argument within the call. Rewrite the onMouseOver event
handler for the image to provide this:

```
<img src="cathedral.jpg" border="2"
➥     onMouseOver="showAlert('A Picture of Seville')"
➥ alt="cathedral" />
```

We'll also rewrite the button's `onClick` event handler to use this function but with a different message:

```
<input type="button" value="Click Here"
➥     onClick="showAlert('Thanks for clicking!')" />
```

Listing 4.4 shows the revised code.

LISTING 4.4   Calling JavaScript Functions from Event Handlers

```
<html>
<head>
<title>A Simple HTML Document</title>
<script language="JavaScript" type="text/javascript">
function showAlert(message)
{
alert(message)
}
</script>
</head>
<body bgcolor="#cccccc">
<center>
<img src="cathedral.jpg" border="2" alt="Cathedral"
➥ onMouseOver="showAlert('A Picture of Seville')" />
<h1>A More Advanced HTML Page</h1>
<h3>Welcome to my second page written in HTML.</h3>
<table border="2">
<tr>
  <th bgcolor="#aaaaaa">Vegetables</th>
  <th bgcolor="#aaaaaa">Fruits</th>
</tr>
<tr>
  <td>Carrot</td>
  <td>Apple</td>
</tr>
<tr>
  <td>Cabbage</td>
  <td>Orange</td>
</tr>
</table><br />
```

```
<p>... and here's some text in a paragraph.</p>
<script language="JavaScript" type="text/javascript">
document.writeln("This line was written using JavaScript!")
</script>
<form>
<input type="button" value="Click Here" onClick=
➥"showAlert('Thanks for clicking!')">
</form>
</center>
</body>
</html>
```

Other Event Handlers

So far you have seen examples of the onClick and onMouseOver event handlers. Many others are available for use; Table 4.1 lists a selection of the most popular event handlers.

TABLE 4.1   Some Common JavaScript Event Handlers

Event Handler	Comments
onChange	Occurs when the value in an input field changes
onClick	Occurs when a user clicks the mouse on the element in question
onLoad	Occurs when the page has finished loading
onMouseOver	Occurs when the mouse pointer enters the screen area occupied by the element in question ...
onMouseOut	... and when it leaves
onSubmit	Occurs at the point a form is submitted

Manipulating Data in JavaScript

You can use JavaScript to achieve much more than popping up dialog boxes. JavaScript gives you the opportunity to define and use variables and arrays, work with date and time arithmetic, and control program flow with loops and conditional branches.

Variables

The concept of a variable might already be familiar to you if you've ever done any algebra, or programmed in just about any computer language. A *variable* is a piece of data given a name by which you can conveniently refer to it later. In JavaScript, you declare variables with the keyword var:

```
var speed = 63;
```

The preceding line of code declares the variable speed and by using the assignment operator = assigns it a value of 63.

We may now use this variable in other statements:

```
var speedlimit = 55;
var speed = 63;
var excess_speed = speed - speedlimit;
```

Variables need not be numeric; the statement

```
var lastname = 'Smith';
```

assigns a string to the variable lastname.

Both numeric and string variables may be manipulated within JavaScript statements. Consider the following code:

```
var firstname = 'Susan';
var lastname = 'Smith';
document.writeln('Hello, '+ firstname + ' ' + lastname);
```

This code would write Hello, Susan Smith into our document.

Objects

You met the concept of an object earlier in the lesson and saw how objects have both properties that describe them and methods that perform actions on them.

Objects in JavaScript have a hierarchical relationship. References begin with the highest-level object, with subsequent levels appended separated by a period:

```
document.image1.src
```

This string starts with the object document, then refers to an object image1 within that object, and finally the property src (the source file for the image).

> **Note** In fact, the object that truly has the highest level in the object hierarchy is window, which refers to the browser screen and everything within it. In general, you don't need to include this object; JavaScript assumes it to be there.

Suppose that we have the following HTML code somewhere in our page:

```
<form name="form1" action="somepage.html" method="post">
<input type="text" name="lastname">
<input type="submit" value="Submit">
</form>
```

We can refer, in JavaScript, to the string that the user has typed into the lastname field by referring to the property value of the object corresponding to that field:

```
document.form1.lastname.value
```

Example—Form Validation

Let's use this technique to check a user's entered form data for validity. We want to trap the event of the user attempting to submit the form and use this event to trigger our JavaScript function, which checks the data for validity. Here's the HTML code for our form:

```
<form name="form1" method="post" action="otherpage.html">
Enter a number from 1 to 10: <input size="4" type="text"
➥     name="usernumber">
<input type="submit" value="Enter"
➥     onSubmit="return numcheck()">
</form>
```

We can see here that the onSubmit event handler is called when the Submit button is clicked and calls a JavaScript function called numcheck(). We need this function to check what our user has entered for validity, and either submit the form or (if the entry is invalid) issue an error. Note the word `return` prior to the function call. This is here because on this occasion we want the function to tell us whether the `submit` method should be allowed to go ahead. We want our function to return a value of `false` to the form if the form submission is to be stopped. Here's the function:

```
<script language="JavaScript" type="text/javascript">
function numcheck()
{
    var numentered = document.form1.usernumber.value;
    if((numentered>=1)&&(numentered<=10))
    {
        return true;
    } else
    {
        alert("Your entry was invalid.  Please try again.");
        return false;
    }
}
```

The first action of the function is to assign the user's entered value to the variable `numentered`. We then test that number for validity by checking that it is greater than or equal to 1 *and* less than or equal to 10. Depending on the result, we either return a value of true to the calling form (thus allowing the form to be submitted) or pop up a dialog informing of the error. In the latter case, when the user clicks OK to clear the dialog, a value of false is returned to the calling form, preventing the form from being submitted until the user enters appropriate data.

Summary

This lesson covered the basics of JavaScript programming. We saw how JavaScript commands may be integrated into HTML pages, discussed grouping JavaScript commands into functions, and learned how event handlers are employed to launch JavaScript commands and functions.

LESSON 5

Server-Side Programming in PHP

Ajax applications can work with virtually any server-side language, requiring only that the server should return correctly formatted responses to its HTTP requests. This lesson introduces PHP, a popular open source scripting language used on a huge number of web servers throughout the world.

Introducing PHP

Like JavaScript, PHP is composed of commands that can be embedded within the HTML code of your pages. PHP however is a server-side programming language—that is, it works hand-in-hand with your web server to process the source code of a page *before* that page is sent to the browser.

Why Do I Need To Know This?

As you are already aware, Ajax applications make calls to the web server and subsequently use the returned information within the page currently being viewed. You need a way to run programs on the server to process the Ajax request and return the required data.

Ajax can work with various server-side technologies including PHP, ASP, Java, and others. This book uses PHP, arguably the most popular and easy to use of the available server-side languages.

This lesson provides an introduction to PHP for those who have never encountered it and a refresher of the basics for any who have.

What Is (and Isn't) Covered in This Lesson

As with every lesson in this part of the book, it is neither feasible nor appropriate to give an exhaustive course on every aspect of the subject.

This lesson covers the basics of PHP programming with some practical examples, concentrating mainly on those aspects of PHP most relevant to our explorations of Ajax.

Tip   The PHP website at http://uk.php.net/ is an invaluable source of information, downloads, and documentation relating to PHP.

Tip   For a much more complete course on PHP, try *Sams Teach Yourself PHP in 24 Hours* by Matt Zandstra.

Embedding PHP in HTML Pages

PHP statements are embedded into HTML documents by surrounding the PHP statements with <?php and ?> tags. Anything between such tags is evaluated by the web server and replaced with appropriate HTML code, prior to the page being served to the browser.

You can have as many sets of <?php and ?> tags in your page as you want.

Tip   Web servers normally recognize by the file extension which files contain PHP code and process them accordingly. The most used file extension for PHP files is .php, but you may also see .php3, .php4, .phtml, and various others. To make your code portable to as many web server environments as possible, it's best to stick with .php.

Outputting HTML from PHP

Several PHP commands can help you write text and HTML code directly into your page. Perhaps the simplest is the echo command:

```
echo "I wrote this line using PHP";
```

The preceding statement simply places "I wrote this line using PHP" into the HTML document at precisely the place where the PHP statement occurs.

Listing 5.1 shows the source code of a PHP file to print Hello World in the browser window.

LISTING 5.1   Printing Hello World in PHP

```
<html>
<head>
<title>A Simple PHP Script</title>
</head>
<body>
<?php echo "<h1>Hello World!</h1>"; ?>
</body>
</html>
```

Note that in this script, the output string also contains some HTML tags, <h1> and </h1>. As the PHP statements are executed by the web server before serving the page to us, these tags are written into the document's HTML along with the "Hello World" text and evaluated by our browser along with all other HTML markup in the document. Figure 5.1 shows the browser displaying our "Hello World" page.

If we ask the browser to show us the source of this page, it displays the following code, in which we can see that the PHP elements have been completely evaluated by the web server, which has inserted the relevant HTML into the page:

```
<html>
<head>
<title>A Simple PHP Script</title>
</head>
<body>
<h1>Hello World!</h1></body>
</html>
```

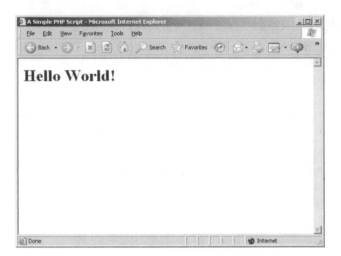

FIGURE 5.1   "Hello World" in PHP.

Variables in PHP

Variables in PHP, much like in any programming language, are named
pockets in which pieces of data are stored. All variable names in PHP
must begin with a "$" character, followed by a string made up of letters,
numbers, and underscores.

Caution   Variable names are case sensitive in PHP. For
example, $varname and $VarName represent two distinct variables. Take care to enter the names of variables in the correct case.

We can assign values to variables in PHP without declaring the variables
beforehand:

```
$score = 71;
$player = 'Harry Scott';
```

Variables can take a number of data types, including strings, integers, floats, and Boolean (true or false). When a variable is assigned a value, such as in the preceding examples, PHP assigns a data type automatically.

Numbers

All the basic mathematical operators are available in PHP, as shown in the following examples:

```
$answer = 13 + 4;
$answer = 13 * 4;
$answer = 13 / 4;
$answer = 13 - 4;
```

You can also calculate the modulus, for which we use the % character:

```
$answer = 13 % 4;
```

Strings

In PHP you enclose strings within single or double quotes:

```
$mystring = "The quick brown fox";
```

Strings may be concatenated using the period character:

```
$newstring = " jumped over the lazy dog";
$concat = $mystring.$newstring;
```

> **Tip** PHP offers the date() command, which allows you to get the server time and date and format it to your liking; for example, the line
>
> ```
> echo date('D F Y H:I');
> ```
>
> outputs the current date in a form similar to Fri 16 December 2005 11:36.

Arrays

PHP also supports arrays. An *array* is a variable that can contain a set of values rather than just one. Here's a PHP array containing some of the days of the week:

```
$daynames = array("Monday","Tuesday","Wednesday",
➥    "Thursday","Friday");
```

The items in an array are referenced by a key, which is an integer starting at zero and incrementing for each item in the array. The following line outputs Thursday to an HTML page:

```
echo $daynames[3];
```

Note that, because the index value begins at zero, the preceding statement actually echoes the fourth element of the array.

This type of array is known as a *numeric array*, but you may also use *associative* arrays. In this case, the key value of each element is not numeric but instead is a string of your choosing. The syntax to declare such an array and assign values to it is slightly different:

```
$lunch = array("Susan" => "Chicken", "Matthew" => "Beef",
➥    "Louise" => "Salmon");
```

You can now select the elements of such an array using the key value:

```
echo $lunch["Louise"];
```

This command would output the word Salmon to our page.

Controlling Program Flow

PHP contains various structures for controlling the flow of your programs. One of the most useful is the simple if statement, which allows you to alter the flow of program execution depending on the outcome of a condition. Let's have a look at a code snippet using the if statement:

```
if($temp > 80)
{
    echo $temp." degrees is too hot.   Turn down
➥        the thermostat.";
}
```

This if statement simply evaluates the condition contained in the brackets. If the condition is satisfied, the statements within the curly braces are executed; otherwise, these statements are ignored.

We can also add an `else` clause to our `if` statement:

```
if($temp > 80)
{
    echo $temp." degrees is too hot.  Turn down
        the thermostat.";
}
else
{
    echo $temp." degrees is cool enough.";
}
```

PHP also has loop constructs, which allow you to repeat the same code instructions a number of times until the conditions are satisfied for the loop to be terminated. This is the code for a `while` loop:

```
$x = 1;
while($x<=12)
{
    echo "This is trip number ".$x." through the loop<br />";
    $x++;
}
```

The statement `$x++` means "increment x by one." The loop executes over and over until the condition

```
$x<=12
```

is no longer met (because `$x` has become greater than 12), and the statements within the curly braces will then be ignored. Program execution then carries on from below the closing curly brace.

You can also make a similar loop using PHP's `for` construct:

```
for($x = 1; $x <= 12; $x++)
{
echo "This is trip number ".$x." through the loop<br />";
}
```

The `for` statement takes an argument with three components. The first is evaluated before the first loop and provides a starting value for `$x`. The second component of the argument is the condition that will be evaluated on each loop to test whether the loop should be executed, and the third is a statement that will be carried out after each loop, and in this case increments `$x`.

The operation of this loop is identical to that of the `while` example.

Summary

This lesson introduced the principles of programming in the PHP server-side language, including the use of variables and program flow control constructs. You have also seen how PHP statements may be embedded into HTML pages.

LESSON 6

A Brief Introduction to XML

The "x" of Ajax stands for XML, a powerful markup language that can allow your Ajax applications to transfer and process complex, structured information. This lesson discusses the basics of creating and using XML documents.

Introducing XML

Anyone who has carried out any HTML markup will already be somewhat familiar with the nature of XML code. XML (eXtensible Markup Language) has many similarities in markup style to HTML.

However, whereas HTML is intended to determine how web pages are displayed, XML has a rather more wide-ranging use. XML documents can be used in all manner of data storage and data exchange applications ranging from document storage and retrieval to roles traditionally fulfilled by database programs.

Why Do I Need To Know This?

One of the many uses of XML is for the transfer of structured information between applications. In Ajax you can use XML to return information from the server to your Ajax application, where it may be parsed and used.

What Is (and Isn't) Covered in This Lesson

In common with the other lessons in this section of the book, we do not attempt to offer a complete and thorough treatise on XML. Rather, this lesson covers the basics of the language and its application, concentrating mainly on those aspects relevant to your work with Ajax.

 Tip   If you want a more in-depth tutorial in XML, see *Sams Teach Yourself XML in 10 Minutes* by Andrew H. Watt.

XML Basics

XML is a markup language that allows data to be stored and transmitted in a structured, hierarchical manner. It has similarities in markup style to HTML, but whereas HTML has a fixed list of element definitions and is designed primarily to allow you to define how a document should be displayed, XML elements may be defined within a particular XML document to suit the data being described there.

In common with HTML, markup elements (normally referred to as *tags*) enclosed by < and > are used to annotate the contents of a text file, describing the information it contains.

Note   The similarities between XML and HTML are not purely accidental. Both are based on SGML (Standard Generalized Markup Language), a system for organizing the elements of a document. SGML was developed and standardized by the International Organization for Standards (ISO).

Unlike the tags in HTML, though, whose definitions are fixed, XML tags can be defined to be anything you want, allowing you to describe virtually any kind of data. Consider this example of an XML document:

```
<race>
  <yacht raceNo='74'>
    <name>Wanderer</name>
    <skipper>Walter Jeffries</skipper>
    <helm>Sally Jacobs</helm>
  </yacht>
```

```
<yacht raceNo='22'>
  <name>Free Spirit</name>
  <skipper>Jennifer Scully</skipper>
  <helm>Paul Thomas</helm>
</yacht>
</race>
```

This short XML document describes a yacht race, including the two competing yachts and their respective personnel. Note how the tag names are descriptive of the data they contain, and how the tag structures are hierarchical. You may also notice that XML tags, like those of HTML, can also have *attributes*. The end effect is that the XML file is quite readable—that is, the meaning of the data may be readily inferred by a human reader.

Caution Unlike HTML, tagnames in XML are case sensitive, so `<yacht>` and `<Yacht>` would be treated as two distinct elements.

Tip XML uses the same syntax as HTML for the display of comments. Any information beginning with the character string `<!--` and ending with the string `-->` will be ignored:

```
<!-- This is a comment -->
```

XML Document Structure

The permitted structure of an XML document has only one mandatory element, the so-called *document element*. In the preceding yacht race example, this would be the `<race>` element.

Note The document element need not necessarily have elements nested within it; the following is an allowable XML document:

```
<competition>Farlington Summer Cup</competition>
```

Document Prolog

Other information may be optionally included before the document element, forming the document's *prolog*. An example is the XML declaration:

```
<?xml version="1.0" ?>
```

> **Caution**   If such a declaration exists, it must be the first thing in the document. Not even white space is allowed before it.

The prolog may also contain, in addition to various comments and processing instructions, a *Document Type Declaration*.

Document Type Declaration

The optional Document Type Declaration (often referred to as a *DOCTYPE declaration*) is a statement of the permitted structure of an XML document. It usually contains (or refers to another file that contains) information about the names of the elements in the document and the relationships between those elements.

> **Caution**   Take care not to confuse the Document Type (DOCTYPE) Declaration with the *Document Type Definition* (DTD). The DTD is comprised of both the markup declarations contained in the DOCTYPE Declaration *and* those contained in any external file to which the DOCTYPE Declaration refers.

Let's look at an example Document Type Declaration for the yacht race document:

```
<!DOCTYPE race SYSTEM race.dtd>
```

This declaration, which would appear in the document before the <race> element, specifies that the document element will be called <race> and that document structure definitions may be found in an external file, `race.dtd`, which would perhaps contain something like the following:

```
<!ELEMENT race (yacht+) >
<!ELEMENT yacht (name, skipper, helm) >
<!ATTLIST yacht raceNo #CDATA #REQUIRED >
<!ELEMENT name (#PCDATA) >
<!ELEMENT skipper (#PCDATA) >
<!ELEMENT helm (#PCDATA) >
```

Alternatively, this information could be quoted in the DOCTYPE Declaration itself, placed between [and] characters:

```
<!DOCTYPE race [
<!ELEMENT race (yacht+) >
<!ATTLIST yacht raceNo #CDATA #REQUIRED >
<!ELEMENT yacht (name, skipper, helm) >
<!ELEMENT name (#PCDATA) >
<!ELEMENT skipper (#PCDATA) >
<!ELEMENT helm (#PCDATA) >
]>
```

In either case we define four *elements*—namely, race, yacht, skipper, and helm—and one *attribute list*.

> **Tip**   DOCTYPE Declarations can contain both internal and external references, known as the *internal and external subsets* of the DTD.

Element Declarations

The line

```
<!ELEMENT race (yacht+) >
```

declares that the `<race>` element will contain elements of type `<yacht>`, whereas the + character indicates that there may be any number of occurrences from one upward of such `<yacht>` elements. Alternatively, we could use the character * to indicate any number of occurrences *including zero*, or the character ? to indicate *zero or one occurrence*. The absence of all of these characters indicates that there should be exactly one `<yacht>` element within `<race>`.

The <yacht> element is declared to contain three further elements, <name>, <skipper>, and <helm>. The #PCDATA term contained in the declarations for those elements stands for *parsed character data* and indicates that these elements must contain character-based data and may not contain further elements. Other possible content types include MIXED (text and elements) and ANY (any valid content).

Attribute List Declarations

Our example also contains the line

```
<!ATTLIST yacht raceNo #CDATA #REQUIRED >
```

Such declarations are used to specify what attributes are permitted or required for any given element. In our example, we specify that the <yacht> element has an attribute called raceNo, the value of which is comprised of #CDATA (character data).

The term #REQUIRED indicates that, in this example, the <yacht> element *must* have such an attribute. Other possibilities include #IMPLIED, specifying that such an attribute is optional; #DEFAULT followed by a value in quotation marks, specifying a default value for the attribute should none be declared in the XML document; or #FIXED followed by a value in quotation marks, fixing the value of the attribute to that quoted.

Valid XML

If an XML document contains a DOCTYPE Declaration and complies fully with the declarations it contains, it is said to be a *valid* XML document.

JavaScript and XML

Most modern browsers already contain some tools to help you deal with XML documents.

A JavaScript object must exist to contain the XML document. Creating a new instance of such an object is done slightly differently depending on whether you use a non-Microsoft browser, such as Mozilla's Firefox, or Microsoft Internet Explorer:

For Firefox and other non-Microsoft browsers, use the following code to create a JavaScript XML document object:

```
<script type="text/javascript">
var myxmlDoc =
    ➥ document.implementation.createDocument("","",null);

myxmlDoc.load("exampleDoc.xml");

Program statements

</script>
```

To create a JavaScript XML document object with Internet Explorer, use this code:

```
<script type="text/javascript">
var myxmlDoc=new ActiveXObject("Microsoft.XMLDOM")
myxmlDoc.async="false"
myxmlDoc.load("exampleDoc.xml")

Program statements

</script>
```

After you have an object to represent the XML document, you may use the properties and methods of that object to gain access to the XML data contained within the document. Effectively, the hierarchical structure and data of the XML document now have equivalents in the JavaScript hierarchy of objects, the Document Object Model (DOM).

The Document Object Model (DOM)

Let's take a look at some of the methods and properties that help you access and manipulate this information, often called *Walking The DOM*.

Nodes

Suppose that our JavaScript object myxmlDoc contains the XML listing of the yacht race. The document element, <race>, contains two elements of type <yacht>; we say it has two *children*.

In general, you can get the number of children belonging to a particular element by using the `childNodes.length` property of the object. Because `<race>` is the document element, it is at the top of the object hierarchy, and we can refer to it simply with the variable `myxmlDoc`:

```
var noYachts = myxmlDoc.childNodes.length;
```

We can also determine information about individual children by appending the node number in parentheses:

```
myxmlDoc.childNode(0)
```

The preceding line refers to the first `<yacht>` element appearing in the document.

Caution   As in many programming constructs, the first element has the number zero, the second element has the number one, and so forth.

We can test for the presence of children for a particular element by using the `hasChildNodes()` method:

```
myxmldoc.childNodes(1).hasChildNodes()
```

This line returns `true` because the second yacht in the document has three children (with tag names `name`, `skipper`, and `helm`). However,

```
myxmldoc.childNodes(1).childNodes(0).hasChildNodes()
```

returns `false` because the `<name>` element within that `<yacht>` element has no children.

Getting Tagnames

The `tagname` property allows you to find the tagname associated with a particular element:

```
myxmldoc.childNodes(0).childNodes(1).tagname
```

The preceding line returns `skipper`.

Getting Element Attributes

The method `getAttribute("AttributeName")` can be used to return the attribute values for a given element:

```
myxmldoc.childNodes(0).getAttribute("raceNo")
```

This line returns 74.

Tag Contents

The `text` property can be used to return the contents of a particular element. The line

```
myxmldoc.childNodes(0).childNodes(1).text
```

would return `Walter Jeffries`.

You'll learn about these and similar methods in more detail in Lesson 14, "Returning Data as XML."

Summary

This lesson discussed the basics of XML, including XML document structures and Document Type Declarations. We also briefly examined how JavaScript may be used to deal with XML data using object properties and methods, much like using any other JavaScript object. This knowledge will be useful when we use Ajax to retrieve XML data from the server.

LESSON 7

Anatomy of an Ajax Application

In this lesson you will learn about the individual building blocks of Ajax and how they fit together to form the architecture of an Ajax application. Subsequent lessons here in Part II, "Introducing Ajax," examine these components in more detail, finally assembling them into a working Ajax application.

The Need for Ajax

In Part I, "A Refresher on Web Technologies," we reviewed the core technologies that form the components of an Ajax application. By now, you will hopefully have at least a rudimentary knowledge of JavaScript, PHP, and XML, all of which we'll use here in Part II.

Before discussing the individual components, let's look in more detail at what we want from our Ajax application.

Traditional Versus Ajax Client-Server Interactions

Lesson 1, "Anatomy of a Website," discussed the traditional page-based model of a website user interface. When you interact with such a website, individual pages containing text, images, data entry forms, and so forth are presented one at a time. Each page must be dealt with individually before navigating to the next.

For instance, you may complete the data entry fields of a form, editing and re-editing your entries as much as you want, knowing that the data will not be sent to the server until the form is finally submitted.

Figure 7.1 illustrates this interaction.

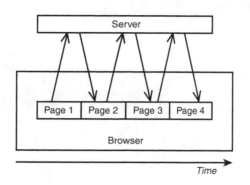

FIGURE 7.1 Traditional client–server interactions.

After you submit a form or follow a navigation link, you then must wait while the browser screen refreshes to display the new or revised page that has been delivered by the server.

As your experience as an Internet user grows, using this interface becomes almost second nature. You learn certain rules of thumb that help to keep you out of trouble, such as "don't press the Submit button a second time," and "don't press the Back button after submitting a form."

Unfortunately, interfaces built using this model have a few drawbacks. First, there is a significant delay while each new or revised page is loaded. This interrupts what we, as users, perceive as the "flow" of the application.

Furthermore, a *whole* page must be loaded on each occasion, even when most of its content is identical to that of the previous page. Items common to many pages on a website, such as header, footer, and navigation sections, can amount to a significant proportion of the data contained in the page.

Figure 7.2 illustrates a website displaying pages before and after the submission of a form, showing how much identical content has been reloaded and how relatively little of the display has actually changed.

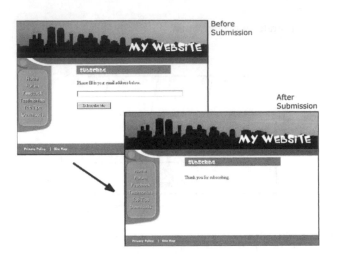

FIGURE 7.2   Many page items are reloaded unnecessarily.

This unnecessary download of data wastes bandwidth and further exacerbates the delay in loading each new page.

> **Note**   *Bandwidth* refers to the capacity of a communications channel to carry information. On the Internet, bandwidth is usually measured in bps (bits per second) or in higher multiples such as Mbps (million bits per second).

The Rich User Experience

The combined effect of the issues just described is to offer a much inferior user experience compared to that provided by the vast majority of desktop applications.

On the desktop, you expect the display contents of a program to remain visible and the interface elements to respond to commands while the computing processes occur quietly in the background. As I write this lesson using a word processor, for example, I can save the document to disk, scroll or page up and down, and alter font faces and sizes without having to wait on each occasion for the entire display to be refreshed.

Ajax allows you to add to your web application interfaces some of this functionality more commonly seen in desktop applications and often referred to as a *rich user experience*.

Introducing Ajax

To improve the user's experience, you need to add some extra capabilities to the traditional page-based interface design. You want your user's page to be interactive, responding to the user's actions with revised content, and be updated without any interruptions for page loads or screen refreshes.

To achieve this, Ajax builds an extra layer of processing between the web page and the server.

This layer, often referred to as an *Ajax Engine* or *Ajax Framework*, intercepts requests from the user and in the background handles server communications quietly, unobtrusively, and *asynchronously*. By this we mean that server requests and responses no longer need to coincide with particular user actions but may happen at any time convenient to the user and to the correct operation of the application. The browser does not freeze and await the completion by the server of the last request but instead lets the user carry on scrolling, clicking, and typing in the current page.

The updating of page elements to reflect the revised information received from the server is also looked after by Ajax, happening dynamically while the page continues to be used.

Figure 7.3 represents how these interactions take place.

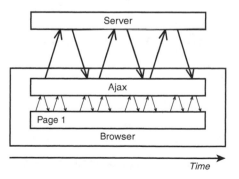

FIGURE 7.3   Ajax client–server interaction.

A Real Ajax Application—Google Suggest

To see an example of an Ajax application in action, let's have a look at *Google Suggest*. This application extends the familiar Google search engine interface to offer the user suggestions for suitable search terms, based on what he has so far typed.

With each key pressed by the user, the application's Ajax layer queries Google's server for suitably similar search phrases and presents the returned data in a drop-down box. Along with each suggested phrase is listed the number of results that would be expected for a search conducted using that phrase. At any point the user has the option to select one of these suggestions instead of continuing to type and have Google process the selected search.

Because the server is queried with every keypress, this drop-down list updates dynamically as the user types—with no waiting for page refreshes or similar interruptions.

Figure 7.4 shows the program in action. You can try it for yourself by following the links from Google's home page at http://www.google.com/webhp?complete=1&hl=en.

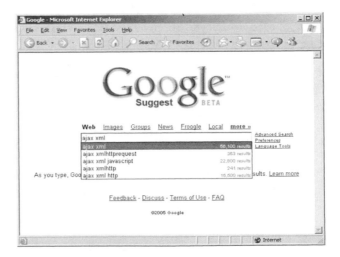

FIGURE 7.4   An example of an Ajax application—Google Suggest.

Next let's identify the individual components of such an Ajax application and see how they work together.

> **Note** Google has presented other Ajax-enabled applications that you can try, including the *gmail* web mail service and the *Google Maps* street mapping program. See the Google website at http://www.google.com/ for details.

The Constituent Parts of Ajax

Now let's examine the components of an Ajax application one at a time.

The XMLHTTPRequest Object

When you click on a hyperlink or submit an HTML form, you send an HTTP request to the server, which responds by serving to you a new or revised page. For your web application to work asynchronously, however, you must have a means to send HTTP requests to the server *without* an associated request to display a new page.

You can do so by means of the XMLHTTPRequest *object*. This JavaScript object is capable of making a connection to the server and issuing an HTTP request without the necessity of an associated page load.

In following lessons you will see how an instance of such an object can be created, and how its properties and methods can be used by JavaScript routines included in the web page to establish asynchronous communications with the server.

> **Tip** As a security measure, the XMLHTTPRequest object can generally only make calls to URLs within the same domain as the calling page and cannot directly call a remote server.

Lesson 8, "The XMLHTPPRequest Object," discusses how to create an instance of the XMLHTTPRequest object and reviews the object's properties and methods.

Talking with the Server

In the traditional style of web page, when you issue a server request via a hyperlink or a form submission, the server accepts that request, carries out any required server-side processing, and subsequently serves to you a new page with content appropriate to the action you have undertaken.

While this processing takes place, the user interface is effectively frozen. You are made quite aware of this, when the server has completed its task, by the appearance in the browser of the new or revised page.

With asynchronous server requests, however, such communications occur in the background, and the completion of such a request does not necessarily coincide with a screen refresh or a new page being loaded. You must therefore make other arrangements to find out what progress the server has made in dealing with the request.

The XMLHTTPRequest object possesses a convenient property to report on the progress of the server request. You can examine this property using JavaScript routines to determine the point at which the server has completed its task and the results are available for use.

Your Ajax armory must therefore include a routine to monitor the status of a request and to act accordingly. We'll look at this in more detail in Lesson 9, "Talking with the Server."

What Happens at the Server?

So far as the server-side script is concerned, the communication from the XMLHTTPRequest object is just another HTTP request. Ajax applications care little about what languages or operating environments exist at the server; provided that the client-side Ajax layer receives a timely and correctly formatted HTTP response from the server, everything will work just fine.

It is possible to build simple Ajax applications with no server-side scripting at all, simply by having the XMLHTTPRequest object call a static server resource such as an XML or text file.

Ajax applications may make calls to various other server-side resources such as web services. Later in the book we'll look at some examples of calling web services using protocols such as SOAP and REST.

> **Note**   In this book we'll be using the popular PHP scripting language for our server-side routines, but if you are more comfortable with ASP, JSP, or some other server-side language, go right ahead and use it in your Ajax applications.

Dealing with the Server Response

Once notified that an asynchronous request has been successfully completed, you may then utilize the information returned by the server.

Ajax allows for this information to be returned in a number of formats, including ASCII text and XML data.

Depending on the nature of the application, you may then translate, display, or otherwise process this information within the current page.

We'll look into these issues in Lesson 10, "Using the Returned Data."

Other Housekeeping Tasks

An Ajax application will be required to carry out a number of other duties too. Examples include detecting error conditions and handling them appropriately, and keeping the user informed about the status of submitted Ajax requests.

You will see various examples in later lessons.

Putting It All Together

Suppose that you want to design a new Ajax application, or update a legacy web application to include Ajax techniques. How do you go about it?

First you need to decide what page events and user actions will be responsible for causing the sending of an asynchronous HTTP request. You may decide, for example, that the onMouseOver event of an image will result in a request being sent to the server to retrieve further information about the subject of the picture; or that the onClick event belonging to a button will generate a server request for information with which to populate the fields on a form.

You saw in Lesson 4, "Client-Side Coding Using JavaScript," how JavaScript can be used to execute instructions on occurrences such as these, by employing event handlers. In your Ajax applications, such methods will be responsible for initiating asynchronous HTTP requests via XMLHTTPRequest.

Having made the request, you need to write routines to monitor the progress of that request until you hear from the server that the request has been successfully completed.

Finally, after receiving notification that the server has completed its task, you need a routine to retrieve the information returned from the server and apply it in the application. You may, for example, want to use the newly returned data to change the contents of the page's body text, populate the fields of a form, or pop open an information window.

Figure 7.5 shows the flow diagram of all this.

In Lesson 11, "Our First Ajax Application," we'll use what we have learned to construct a complete Ajax application.

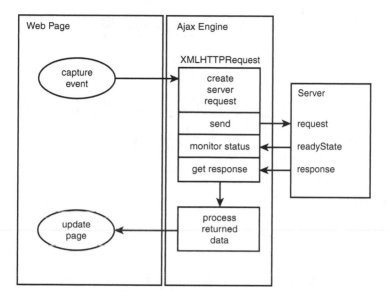

FIGURE 7.5   How the components of an Ajax application work together.

Summary

This lesson discussed the shortcomings of the traditional web interface, identifying specific problems we want to overcome. We also introduced the various building blocks of an Ajax application and discussed how they work together.

In the following lessons of Part II, we will look at these components in more detail, finally using them to build a complete Ajax application.

LESSON 8

The XMLHTTPRequest Object

In this lesson you will learn how to create an instance of the XMLHTTPRequest *object regardless of which browser your user may have. The object's properties and methods will be introduced.*

More About JavaScript Objects

Lesson 7, "Anatomy of an Ajax Application," introduced the building blocks of an Ajax application and discussed how these pieces fit together.

This lesson examines the object at the heart of every Ajax application—the XMLHTTPRequest object.

> **Note** You briefly met *objects* in Lesson 4, "Client-Side Coding Using JavaScript," when we discussed the document object associated with a web page. The XMLHTTPRequest object, after it has been created, becomes a further such object within the page's object hierarchy and has its own properties and methods.

An object can be thought of as a single package containing a set of *properties*, which contain and classify data, and a set of *methods* with which the object can perform actions on that data.

Suppose, for example, that we had an object of type wheelbarrow. Such an object might have a property contents, which describes how many items the wheelbarrow holds at any given moment. Methods might include `fill()`, `tip()`, `forward()`, and `stop()`. When using JavaScript you can design such objects as you see fit.

However, in addition to user-defined objects, JavaScript has a range of ready-made objects for use in scripts. These are referred to as *native* objects. Examples of JavaScript's native objects include `Math()`, `String()`, and `Date()`.

Creating an Instance of an Object

Many objects, such as the document object that you saw in Lesson 4, already exist and therefore do not need you to create an instance of them. Others, however, require you to create an instance of the object in question before you can use it.

You can create an instance of an object by calling a method known as the object's *constructor*, using the new keyword:

```
var myBarrow = new Wheelbarrow();
```

Having created an instance myBarrow of the object wheelbarrow, properties and methods for the object may be manipulated using a simple syntax:

```
myBarrow.contents = 20;
myBarrow.forward();
myBarrow.stop();
myBarrow.tip();
```

Of course, you are at liberty to create other instances of the same object and have them exist concurrently:

```
var myBarrow = new Wheelbarrow();
var yourBarrow = new Wheelbarrow();
myBarrow.contents = 20;
yourBarrow.contents = 50;
```

The Document Object Model or DOM

We mentioned briefly in Lesson 4 the hierarchy of objects "built in" to a web page and known as the *Document Object Model*. You access these objects and their properties and methods in the same way as native objects and objects that you devise and create yourself.

> **Note** The Document Object Model or DOM is really not a part of JavaScript but a separate entity existing outside it. Although you can use JavaScript to manipulate DOM objects, other scripting languages may equally well access them too.

In later lessons you'll see how the XMLHTTPRequest object can use XML data returned from the server in response to XMLHTTPRequest calls to create additional DOM objects that you can use in your scripts.

Introducing XMLHTTPRequest

XMLHTTPRequest is supported by virtually all modern browsers, including Microsoft's Internet Explorer 5+ and a variety of non-Microsoft browsers, including Mozilla, Firefox, Konqueror, Opera, and Safari, and is supported on a wide range of platforms, including Microsoft Windows, UNIX/Linux, and Mac OS X.

> **Caution** Some browsers may require attention to their security settings to allow the XMLHTTPRequest object to operate correctly. See your browser's documentation for details.

The purpose of the XMLHTTPRequest object is to allow JavaScript to formulate HTTP requests and submit them to the server. Traditionally programmed web applications normally make such requests *synchronously*, in conjunction with a user-initiated event such as clicking on a link or submitting a form, resulting in a new or updated page being served to the browser.

Using XMLHTTPRequest, however, you can have your page make such calls *asynchronously* in the background, allowing you to continue using the page without the interruption of a browser refresh and the loading of a new or revised page.

This capability underpins all Ajax applications, making the XMLHTTPRequest object the key to Ajax programming.

> **Tip** Although the object's name begins with *XML*, in fact, any type of document may be returned from the server; ASCII text, HTML, and XML are all popular choices, and we will encounter all of these in the course of the book.

Creating the XMLHTTPRequest Object

You cannot make use of the XMLHTTPRequest until you have created an instance of it. Creating an instance of an object in JavaScript is usually just a matter of making a call to a method known as the object's constructor. In the case of XMLHTTPRequest, however, you must change this routine a little to cater for the peculiarities of different browsers, as you see in the following section.

Different Rules for Different Browsers

Microsoft first introduced the XMLHTTPRequest object, implementing it in Internet Explorer 5 as an *ActiveX object*.

> **Tip** ActiveX is a proprietary Microsoft technology for enabling active objects into web pages. Among the available web browsers, it is currently only supported in Microsoft's Internet Explorer. Internet Explorer uses its built-in XML parser, MSXML, to create the XMLHTTPRequest object.

Most other browser developers have now included into their products an equivalent object, but implemented as a native object in the browser's JavaScript interpreter.

Because you don't know in advance which browser, version, or operating system your users will have, your code must adapt its behavior on-the-fly to ensure that the instance of the object will be created successfully.

For the majority of browsers that support XMLHTTPRequest as a native object (Mozilla, Opera, and the rest), creating an instance of this object is straightforward. The following line creates an XMLHTTPRequest object called request:

```
var request = new XMLHTTPRequest();
```

Here we have declared a variable request and assigned to it the value returned from the statement new XMLHTTPRequest(), which is invoking the constructor method for the XMLHTTPRequest object.

To achieve the equivalent result in Microsoft Internet Explorer, you need to create an ActiveX object. Here's an example:

```
var request = new ActiveXObject("Microsoft.XMLHTTP");
```

Once again, this assigns the name request to the new object.

To complicate matters a little more, some versions of Internet Explorer have a different version of MSXML, the Microsoft XML parser, installed; in those cases you need to use the following instruction:

```
var request = new ActiveXObject("Msxml2.XMLHTTP");
```

A Solution for All Browsers

You need, therefore, to create a script that will correctly create an instance of a XMLHTTPRequest object regardless of which browser you are using (provided, of course, that the browser supports XMLHTTPRequest).

A good solution to this problem is to have your script try in turn each method of creating an instance of the object, until one such method succeeds. Have a look at Listing 8.1, in which such a strategy is used.

LISTING 8.1   Using Object Detection for a Cross-Browser Solution

```
function getXMLHTTPRequest()
{
var request = false;
try
  {
    request = new XMLHttpRequest(); /* e.g. Firefox */
  }
catch(err1)
  {
  try
    {
    vrequest = new ActiveXObject("Msxml2.XMLHTTP");
  /* some versions IE */
    }
  catch(err2)
    {
    try
      {
      request = new ActiveXObject("Microsoft.XMLHTTP");
  /* some versions IE */
      }
      catch(err3)
        {
        request = false;
        }
      }
    }
  return request;
  }
```

Listing 8.1 uses the JavaScript statements try and catch. The try statement allows us to attempt to run a piece of code. If the code runs without errors, all is well; however, should an error occur we can use the catch statement to intervene before an error message is sent to the user and determine what the program should then do about the error.

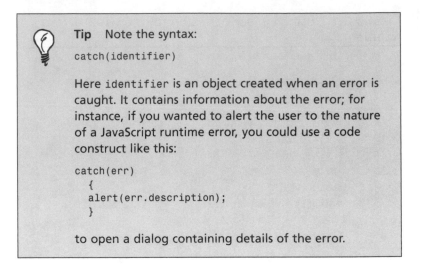

Tip   Note the syntax:

```
catch(identifier)
```

Here identifier is an object created when an error is caught. It contains information about the error; for instance, if you wanted to alert the user to the nature of a JavaScript runtime error, you could use a code construct like this:

```
catch(err)
  {
  alert(err.description);
  }
```

to open a dialog containing details of the error.

An alternative, and equally valid, technique would be to detect which type of browser is in use by testing which objects are defined in the browser. Listing 8.2 shows this technique.

LISTING 8.2   Using Browser Detection for a Cross-Browser Solution

```
function getXMLHTTPRequest()
{
var request = false;
if(window.XMLHTTPRequest)
   {
   request = new XMLHTTPRequest();
   } else {
   if(window.ActiveXObject)
     {
     try
         {
         request = new ActiveXObject("Msml2.XMLHTTP");
         }
     catch(err1)
         {
         try
             {
                   request =
new ActiveXObject("Microsoft.XMLHTTP");
```

```
                }
            catch(err2)
                {
                request = false;
                }
            }
        }
    }
    return request;
    }
```

In this example we've used the test

```
if(window.XMLHTTPRequest) { ... }
```

to determine whether XMLHTTPRequest is a native object of the browser in use; if so, we use the constructor method

```
request = new XMLHTTPRequest();
```

to create an instance of the XMLHTTPRequest object; otherwise, we try creating a suitable ActiveX object as in the first example.

Whatever method you use to create an instance of the XMLHTTPRequest object, you should be able to call this function like this:

```
var myRequest = getXMLHTTPRequest();
```

> **Note** JavaScript also makes available a navigator object that holds information about the browser being used to view the page. Another method we could have used to branch our code is to use this object's appName property to find the name of the browser:
>
> ```
> var myBrowser = navigator.appName;
> ```
>
> This would return "Microsoft Internet Explorer" for IE.

Methods and Properties

Now that we have created an instance of the XMLHTTPRequest object, let's look at some of the object's properties and methods, listed in Table 8.1.

TABLE 8.1   XMLHTTPRequest Objects and Methods

Properties	Description
onreadystatechange	Determines which event handler will be called when the object's readyState property changes
readyState	Integer reporting the status of the request: 0 = uninitialized 1 = loading 2 = loaded 3 = interactive 4 = completed
responseText	Data returned by the server in text string form
responseXML	Data returned by the server expressed as a document object
status	HTTP status code returned by server
statusText	HTTP reason phrase returned by server

Methods	Description
abort()	Stops the current request
getAllResponseHeaders()	Returns all headers as a string
getResponseHeader(x)	Returns the value of header x as a string
open('method', 'URL','a')	specifies the HTTP method (for example, GET or POST), the target URL, and whether the request should be handled asynchronously (If yes, a='true'—the default; if no, a='false'.)
send(content)	Sends the request, optionally with POST data
setRequestHeader ('x','y')	Sets a parameter and value pair x=y and assigns it to the header to be sent with the request

Over the next few lessons we'll examine how these methods and properties are used to create the functions that form the building blocks of Ajax applications.

For now, let's examine just a few of these methods.

The open() Method

The open() method prepares the XMLHTTPRequest object to communicate with the server. You need to supply at least the two mandatory arguments to this method:

- First, specify which HTTP method you intend to use, usually GET or POST. (The use of GET and POST HTTP requests was discussed in Lesson 3, "Sending Requests Using HTTP.")

- Next, the destination URL of the request is included as the second argument. If making a GET request, this URL needs to be suitably encoded with any parameters and their values as part of the URL.

For security reasons, the XMLHTTPRequest object is allowed to communicate only with URLs within its own domain. An attempt to connect to a remote domain results in a "permission denied" error message.

> **Caution** A common mistake is to reference your domain as mydomain.com in a call made from www.mydomain.com. The two will be regarded as different by the JavaScript interpreter, and connection will not be allowed.

Optionally you may include a third argument to the send request, a Boolean value to declare whether the request is being sent in asynchronous mode. If set to false, the request will not be sent in asynchronous mode, and the page will be effectively locked until the request is completed. The default value of true will be assumed if the parameter is omitted, and requests will then be sent asynchronously.

> **Note**   A Boolean data type has only two possible val-
> ues, 1 (or `true`) and 0 (or `false`).

The `send()` Method

Having prepared the `XMLHTTPRequest` using the `open()` method, you can
send the request using the `send()` method. One argument is accepted by
the `send()` function.

If your request is a `GET` request, the request information will be encoded
into the destination URL, and you can then simply invoke the `send()`
method using the argument `null`:

```
objectname.send(null);
```

However, if you are making a `POST` request, the content of the request
(suitably encoded) will be passed as the argument.

```
objectname.setRequestHeader('Content-Type',
➥'application/x-www-form-urlencoded');
objectname.send(var1=value1&var2=value2);
```

In this case we use the `setRequestHeader` method to indicate what type
of content we are including.

Summary

This lesson introduced the `XMLHTTPRequest` object, the driving force
behind any Ajax application, and illustrated how an instance of such an
object is created both for Internet Explorer and for other, non-Microsoft
browsers. We also briefly examined some of the object's properties and
methods.

Following lessons will show how more of the object's methods and properties are used.

LESSON 9
Talking with the Server

In this lesson you'll learn how to use the properties and methods of the XMLHTTPRequest *object to allow the object to send requests to and receive data from the server.*

Sending the Server Request

Lesson 8, "The XMLHTTPRequest Object," discussed at some length the JavaScript XMLHTTPRequest object and how an instance of it may be created in various different browsers.

Now that we have our XMLHTTPRequest object, let's consider how to create and send server requests, and what messages we might expect to receive back from the server.

We're going to jump right in and first write some code using what you learned in Lesson 8 to create an XMLHTTPRequest object called myRequest. We'll then write a JavaScript function called callAjax() to send an asynchronous request to the server using that object. Afterward we'll break down the code line by line to see what it's doing.

Listing 9.1 shows our prototype function to prepare and send an Ajax request using this object.

LISTING 9.1 Sending a Server Request

```
function getXMLHTTPRequest()
{
var req = false;
try
  {
```

continues

LISTING 9.1   Continued

```
    req = new XMLHttpRequest(); /* e.g. Firefox */
  }
catch(err1)
  {
  try
    {
     req = new ActiveXObject("Msxml2.XMLHTTP");
  /* some versions IE */
    }
  catch(err2)
    {
    try
      {
       req = new ActiveXObject("Microsoft.XMLHTTP");
  /* some versions IE */
      }
      catch(err3)
        {
         req = false;
        }
    }
  }
return req;
}

var myRequest = getXMLHTTPRequest();

function callAjax() {
// declare a variable to hold some information
// to pass to the server
var lastname = 'Smith';
// build the URL of the server script we wish to call
var url = "myserverscript.php?surname=" + lastname;
// ask our XMLHTTPRequest object to open a
// server connection
myRequest.open("GET", url, true);
// prepare a function responseAjax() to run when
// the response has arrived
myRequest.onreadystatechange = responseAjax;
// and finally send the request
myRequest.send(null);
}
```

> **Tip**   Lines starting with // are treated as comments by JavaScript. You may use lines like these to document your code or add other useful notes, and your browser's JavaScript interpreter will ignore them when executing code instructions.

First, we need to create an instance of an XMLHTTPRequest object and call it myRequest. You'll no doubt recognize the code for this from Lesson 8.

Next we'll look at the function callAjax().

The first line simply declares a variable and assigns a value to it:

```
var lastname = 'Smith';
```

This is the piece of data that our function intends to send to the server, as the value of a variable called surname that is required by our server-side script. In reality, of course, the value of such data would usually be obtained dynamically by handling a page event such as a mouse click or a keyboard entry, but for now this will serve as a simple example.

The server request we intend to make is a GET request, so we must construct a suitable target URL having our parameter and value pairs suitably coded on the end; the next line carries this out:

```
var url = "myserverscript.php?surname=" + lastname;
```

We dealt briefly with the open() method in Lesson 8. We use it in the next line to prepare our server request:

```
myRequest.open("GET", url, true);
```

This line specifies that we are preparing a GET request and passes to it the destination URL complete with the appended content of the GET request.

The third parameter, true, indicates that we want our request to be handled asynchronously. In this case it could have been omitted because the default value of true is assumed in such cases. However, it does no harm to include it for clarity.

Next, we need to tell our `XMLHTTPRequest` object `myRequest` what it should do with the "progress reports" it will receive from the server. The `XMLHTTPRequest` object has a property `onreadystatechange` that contains information about what JavaScript function should be called whenever the server status changes, and in the next line

```
myRequest.onreadystatechange = responseAjax;
```

we assign the function `responseAjax()` to do this job. We will write this function later in the lesson.

Dealing with the Browser Cache

All browsers maintain a so-called *cache* of visited web pages, a local record of page contents stored on the hard disk of the browser's computer. When you request a particular web page, the browser first tries to load the page from its cache, rather than submitting a new HTTP request.

> **Note** This appears to be more of a problem with IE than with the non-Microsoft browsers. Only GET requests are affected; POST requests are not cached.

Although this can sometimes be advantageous in terms of page load times, it creates a difficulty when trying to write Ajax applications. Ajax is all about talking to the server, not reloading information from cache; so when you make an asynchronous request to the server, a new HTTP request must be generated every time.

It is possible to add HTTP headers to the data returned by server-side routines, intended to tell the browser not to cache a particular page. Examples include

```
"Pragma: no-cache"
```

and

```
"Cache-Control: must-revalidate"
```

among others.

Unfortunately such strategies vary widely in their effectiveness. Different browsers have different cache handling strategies and support different header declarations, making it difficult to ensure that pages are not cached.

A commonly used trick to work around this problem involves the adding of a parameter with a random and meaningless value to the request data. In the case of a GET request, this necessitates adding a further parameter and value pair to the end of the URL.

If the random part of the URL is different each time, this effectively "fools" the browser into believing that it is to send the asynchronous request to an address not previously visited. This results in a new HTTP request being sent on every occasion.

Let's see how to achieve this. In JavaScript, you can generate random numbers using the Math.random() method of the native Math() object. Listing 9.2 contains a couple of changes to our callAjax() function.

LISTING 9.2   Dealing with the Browser Cache

```
function getXMLHTTPRequest()
{
var req = false;
try
  {
    req = new XMLHttpRequest(); /* e.g. Firefox */
  }
catch(err1)
  {
  try
    {
      req = new ActiveXObject("Msxml2.XMLHTTP");
  /* some versions IE */
    }
  catch(err2)
    {
    try
      {
        req = new ActiveXObject("Microsoft.XMLHTTP");
  /* some versions IE */
      }
```

continues

LISTING 9.2 Continued

```
      catch(err3)
        {
          req = false;
        }
    }
  }
return req;
}

var myRequest = getXMLHTTPRequest();

function callAjax() {
// declare a variable to hold some information
// to pass to the server
var lastname = 'Smith';
// build the URL of the server script we wish to call
var url = "myserverscript.php?surname=" + lastname;
// generate a random number
var myRandom=parseInt(Math.random()*99999999);
// ask our XMLHTTPRequest object to open
// a server connection
myRequest.open("GET", url + "&rand=" + myRandom, true);
// prepare a function responseAjax() to run when
// the response has arrived
myRequest.onreadystatechange = responseAjax;
// and finally send the request
myRequest.send(null);
}
```

We can see from Listing 9.2 that the script will now generate a destination URL for our Ajax request that looks something like this:

```
myserverscript.php?surname=Smith&rand=XXXX
```

where XXXX will be some random number, thereby preventing the page from being returned from cache and forcing a new HTTP request to be sent to the server.

> **Note** Some programmers prefer to add the current timestamp rather than a random number. This is a string of characters derived from the current date and time. In the following example, the JavaScript `Date()` and `getTime()` methods of the native `Date()` object are used:
>
> ```
> myRand= + new Date().getTime()
> ```

Monitoring Server Status

The XMLHTTPRequest object contains mechanisms by which we can stay informed of the progress of our Ajax request and determine when the information returned by the server is ready to use in our application.

Let's now have a look at the relevant properties.

The readyState Property

The readyState property of the XMLHTTPRequest object gives you information from the server about the current state of a request you have made. This property is monitored by the onreadystatechange property, and changes in the value of readyState cause onreadystatechange to become true and therefore cause the appropriate function (responseAjax() in our example) to be executed.

> **Tip** The function called on completion of the server request is normally referred to as the *callback function*.

readyState can take the following values:

   0 = uninitialized

   1 = loading

2 = loaded

3 = interactive

4 = completed

When a server request is first made, the value of readyState is set to zero, meaning uninitialized.

As the server request progresses, data begins to be loaded by the server into the XMLHTTPRequest object, and the value of the readyState property changes accordingly, moving to 1 and then 2.

An object readyState value of 3, interactive, indicates that the object is sufficiently progressed so that certain interactivity with it is possible, though the process is not yet fully complete.

When the server request has completed fully and the object is available for further processing, the value of readyState changes finally to 4.

 Tip   Not all of the possible values may exist for any given object. The object may "skip" certain states if they bear no relevance to the object's content type.

In most practical cases, you should look for the readyState property to achieve a value of 4, at which point you can be assured that the server has finished its task and the XMLHTTPRequest object is ready for use.

Server Response Status Codes

In addition to the readyState property, you have a further means to check that an asynchronous request has executed correctly: the HTTP server response status code.

HTTP responses were discussed in Lesson 3, "Sending Requests Using HTTP." If you refer to Table 3.1 you'll see that a response status code of 200 corresponds to an OK message from the server.

We'll see how to test for this as we further develop our callback function.

The Callback Function

By now, then, you have learned how to create an instance of an XMLHTTPRequest object, declare the identity of a callback function, and prepare and send an asynchronous server request. You also know which property tells you when the server response is available for use.

Let's look at our callback function, responseAjax().

First, note that this function is called every time there is a change in the value of the onreadystatechange property. Usually, then, when this function is called, it is required to do absolutely nothing because the value of the readyState property has not yet reached 4 and we therefore know that the server request has not completed its processing.

We can achieve this simply by using a JavaScript if statement:

```
function responseAjax() {
    // we are only interested in readyState of 4,
    // i.e. "completed"
    if(myRequest.readyState == 4) {
        … program execution statements …
    }
}
```

In addition to checking that the server request has completed, we also want to check the HTTP response status code to ensure that it is equal to 200, indicating a successful response to our asynchronous HTTP request.

Referring quickly back to Table 8.1, we can see that our XMLHTTPRequest object myRequest has two properties that report the HTTP status response. These are

```
myRequest.status
```

which contains the status response code, and

```
myRequest.statusText
```

containing the reason phrase.

We can employ these properties by using a further loop:

```
function responseAjax() {
    // we are only interested in readyState of 4,
```

```
      // i.e. "loaded"
      if(myRequest.readyState == 4) {
          // if server HTTP response is "OK"
          if(myRequest.status == 200) {
              … program execution statements …
          } else {
              // issue an error message for any
              // other HTTP response
              alert("An error has occurred: "
➥+ myRequest.statusText);
          }
      }
}
```

This code introduces an else clause into our if statement. Any server status response other than 200 causes the contents of this else clause to be
executed, opening an alert dialog containing the text of the reason phrase
returned from the server.

Using the Callback Function

So how do we go about calling our callAjax() function from our HTML
page? Let's see an example. Here's the code for a simplified form in an
HTML page:

```
<form name='form1'>
Name: <input type='text' name='myname'><br>
Tel: <input type='text' name='telno'><br>
<input type='submit'>
</form>
```

We'll launch the function using the onBlur event handler of a text input
field in a form:

```
<form name='form1'>
Name: <input type='text' name='myname'
➥onBlur='callAjax()'><br>
Tel: <input type='text' name='telno'><br>
<input type='submit'>
</form>
```

The onBlur event handler is activated when the user leaves the field in question. In this case, when the user leaves the field, callAjax() will be executed, creating an instance of the XMLHTTPRequest object and making an asynchronous server request to

```
myserverscript.php?surname=Smith
```

That doesn't sound very useful. However, what if we were to now make a slight change to the code of callAjax()?

```
function callAjax() {
// declare a variable to hold some
// information to pass to the server
var lastname = document.form1.myname.value;
…..
```

Now we can see that, as the user leaves the form field myname, the value she had typed into that field would be passed to the server via our asynchronous request. Such a call may, for example, check a database to verify the existence of the named person, and if so return information to populate other fields on the form.

The result, so far as the user is concerned, is that she sees the remaining fields magically populated with data before submitting—or even completing—the form.

How we might use the returned data to achieve such a result is discussed in Lesson 10, "Using the Returned Data."

Summary

This lesson looked at the ways in which our XMLHTTPRequest object can communicate with the server, including sending asynchronous requests, monitoring the server status, and executing a callback function.

In Lesson 10, you will see how Ajax applications can deal with the data returned by the server request.

LESSON 10
Using the Returned Data

In this lesson you will learn how to process the information returned from the server in response to an Ajax request.

The `responseText` and `responseXML` Properties

Lesson 9, "Talking with the Server," discussed the server communications that allow you to send and monitor asynchronous server requests. The final piece of the Ajax jigsaw is the information returned by the server in response to a request.

This lesson discusses what forms that information can take, and how you can process it and use it in an application. We will use two of the `XMLHTTPRequest` object's properties, namely `responseText` and `responseXML`.

Table 8.1 listed several properties of the `XMLHTTPRequest` object that we have yet to describe. Among these are the `responseText` and `responseXML` properties.

Lesson 9 discussed how we could use the `readyState` property of the `XMLHTTPRequest` object to determine the current status of the `XMLHTTPRequest` call. By the time our server request has completed, as detected by the condition `myRequest.readyState == 4` for our `XMLHTTPRequest` object `myRequest`, then the two properties `responseText` and `responseXML` will respectively contain text and XML representations of the data returned by the server.

In this lesson you'll see how to access the information contained in these two properties and apply each in an Ajax application.

The `responseText` Property

The `responseText` property tries to represent the information returned by the server as a text string.

 Tip If the `XMLHTTPRequest` call fails with an error, or has not yet been sent, `responseText` will have a value `null`.

Let's look again at the callback function prototype:

```
function responseAjax() {
    // we are only interested in readyState of 4, i.e. "loaded"
    if(myRequest.readyState == 4) {
        // if server HTTP response is "OK"
        if(myRequest.status == 200) {
            … program execution statements …
        } else {
            // issue an error message for any other HTTP
➡response
            alert("An error occurred: " + myRequest.statusText);
        }
    }
}
```

Let's add a program statement to the branch of the `if` statement that is executed on success, as in Listing 10.1.

LISTING 10.1 Displaying the Value of `responseText`

```
function responseAjax() {
    // we are only interested in readyState of 4,
    // i.e. "completed"
    if(myRequest.readyState == 4) {
        // if server HTTP response is "OK"
        if(myRequest.status == 200) {
            alert("The server said: "
➡+ myRequest.responseText);
        } else {
            // issue an error message for
            // any other HTTP response
            alert("An error has occurred: "
```

continues

LISTING 10.1   Continued

```
+ myRequest.statusText);
        }
    }
}
```

In this simple example, our script opens an alert dialog to display the text returned by the server. The line

```
alert("The server said: " + myRequest.responseText);
```

takes the text returned by the server-side routine and appends it to the string "The server said: " before presenting it in a JavaScript alert dialog.

Let's look at an example using a simple PHP file on the server:

```
<?php echo "Hello Ajax caller!"; ?>
```

A successful XMLHTTPRequest call to this file would result in the responseText property containing the string Hello Ajax caller!, causing the callback function to produce the dialog shown in Figure 10.1.

![Microsoft Internet Explorer dialog box with warning icon showing the text "The server said: Hello Ajax caller!" and an OK button]

FIGURE 10.1   Output generated by Listing 10.1.

Caution   The responseText property is read-only, so there's no point in trying to manipulate its value until that value has first been copied into another variable.

Because the responseText contains a simple text string, we can manipulate it using any of JavaScript's methods relating to strings. Table 10.1 includes some of the available methods.

TABLE 10.1 Some JavaScript String Manipulation Methods

Method	Description
charAt(*number*)	Selects the single character at the specified position within the string
indexOf(*substring*)	Finds the position where the specified substring starts
lastIndexOf(*substring*)	Finds the last occurrence of the substring within the string
substring(*start*,*end*)	Gets the specified part of the string
toLowerCase()	Converts the string to lowercase
toUpperCase()	Converts the string to uppercase

We'll be looking at how responseText may be used in real situations in Lesson 12, "Returning Data as Text," and Lesson 13, "AHAH—Asynchronous HTML and HTTP."

The responseXML Property

Now suppose that the PHP script we used on the server in the previous example had instead looked like Listing 10.2.

LISTING 10.2 A Server-Side Script to Return XML

```php
<?php
header('Content-Type: text/xml');
echo "<?xml version=\"1.0\" ?><greeting>
➥Hello Ajax caller!</greeting>";
?>
```

Although this is a short script, it is worthwhile to look at it in some detail.

The first line inside the <?php and ?> delimiters uses PHP's header instruction to add an HTTP header to the returned data.

Caution Make sure that your PHP script does not output anything—even white space characters such as spaces and line returns—prior to issuing a header() instruction; otherwise, an error will occur.

The header returned is the parameter and value pair

```
Content-Type: text/xml
```

which announces to our XMLHTTPRequest object to expect that the following data from the server will be formatted as XML.

The next line is a PHP echo statement that outputs this simple, but complete, XML document:

```
<?xml version="1.0" ?>
<greeting>
Hello Ajax caller!
</greeting>
```

Note In PHP you need to escape any quotes that occur within a quoted string to ensure that the meaning of the statement is unambiguous. You do so using a backslash character, hence the PHP command

```
echo "<img src=\"picture.gif\">";
```

produces the output:

```
<img src="picture.gif">
```

When the server call is completed, we now find this XML document loaded into the responseXML property of our XMLHTTPRequest object.

> **Tip** It is important to note that the responseXML property does not contain just a string that forms a text representation of the XML document, as was the case with the responseText property; instead, the entire data and hierarchical structure of the XML document has been stored as a DOM-compatible object.

We can now access the content of the XML document via JavaScript's DOM methods and properties.

Another Useful JavaScript DOM Property

You will no doubt recall that we described some of these methods in Lesson 6, "A Brief Introduction to XML." Let's now examine one more of these methods, namely getElementsByTagName().

The getElementsByTagName() Method

This useful method allows you to build a JavaScript array of all the elements having a particular tagname. You can then access elements of that array using normal JavaScript statements. Here's an example:

```
var myElements = object.getElementsByTagName('greeting');
```

This line creates the array myElements and populates it with all the elements with tagname greeting. As with any other array, you can find out the length of the array (that is, the number of elements having the declared tagname) by using the length property:

```
myElements.length
```

You can access a particular element individually if you want; the first occurring element with tagname greeting can be accessed as myElements[0], the second (if there is a second) as myElements[1], and so:

```
var theElement = myElements[0];
```

> **Tip**   You could also access these individual array elements directly:
>
> ```
> var theElement = object.getElementsByTagName
> ➥('greeting')[0];
> ```

Parsing responseXML

Listing 10.3 gives an example of how we can use
getElementsByTagName(), alongside some other methods discussed in
Lesson 6, to return the text of our greeting in an alert dialog.

LISTING 10.3   Parsing responseXML using
getElementsByTagName()

```
function responseAjax() {
    // we are only interested in readyState
    // of 4, i.e. "completed"
    if(myRequest.readyState == 4) {
        // if server HTTP response is "OK"
        if(myRequest.status == 200) {
            var greetNode = http.responseXML
➥.getElementsByTagName("greeting")[0];
            var greetText = greetNode.childNodes[0]
➥.nodeValue;
            alert("Greeting text: " + greetText);
        } else {
            // issue an error message for
            // any other HTTP response
            alert("An error has occurred: "
➥+ myRequest.statusText);
        }
    }
}
```

After the usual checks on the values of the readyState and status properties, the code locates the required element from responseXML using the
getElementsByTagName() method and then uses
childNodes[0].nodeValue to extract the text content from this element,
finally displaying the returned text in a JavaScript alert dialog.

Figure 10.2 shows the alert dialog, showing the text string recovered from the <greeting> element of the XML document.

Greeting text: Hello Ajax caller!

FIGURE 10.2 Displaying the returned greeting.

Providing User Feedback

In web pages with traditional interfaces, it is clear to the user when the server is busy processing a request; the interface is effectively unusable while a new page is being prepared and served.

The situation is a little different in an Ajax application. Because the interface remains usable during an asynchronous HTTP request, it may not be apparent to the user that new information is expected from the server. Fortunately there are some simple ways to warn that a server request in is progress.

Recall that our callback function is called each time the value of readyState changes, but that we are only really interested in the condition myRequest.readyState == 4, which indicates that the server request is complete.

Let's refer again to Listing 10.3. For all values of readyState other than 4, the function simply terminates having done nothing. We can use these changes to the value of readyState to indicate to the user that a server request is progressing but has not yet completed. Consider the following code:

```
function responseAjax() {
    if(myRequest.readyState == 4) {
        if(myRequest.status == 200) {
            … [success - process the server response]   …
        } else {
            … [failed - report the HTTP error]   …
```

```
        }
    } else {        // if readyState has changed
                    // but readyState <> 4
        … [do something here to provide user feedback] …
    }
}
```

A commonly used way to do this is to modify the contents of a page element to show something eye-catching, such as a flashing or animated graphic, while a request is being processed and then remove it when processing is complete.

The `getElementById()` Method

JavaScript's `getElementById()` method allows you to locate an individual document element by its `id` value. You can use this method in your user feedback routine to temporarily change the contents of a particular page element to provide the visual clue that a server request is in progress.

> **Tip** Elements within a page that have had `id` values declared are expected to each have a unique `id` value. This allows you to identify a unique element. Contrast this with the `class` attribute, which can be applied to any number of separate elements in a page and is more commonly used to set the display characteristics of a group of objects.

Suppose that we have, say, a small animated graphic file `anim.gif` that we want to display while awaiting information from the server. We want to display this graphic inside a `<div>` element within the HTML page. We begin with this `<div>` element empty:

```
<div id="waiting"></div>
```

Now consider the code of the callback function:

```
function responseAjax() {
    if(myRequest.readyState == 4) {
        document.getElementById('waiting').innerHTML = '';
```

```
        if(myRequest.status == 200) {
              … [success - process the server response]   …
        } else {
              … [failed - report the HTTP error]   …
        }
    } else {       // if readyState has changed
                   // but readyState <> 4
           document.getElementById('waiting')
➥.innerHTML = '<img src="anim.gif">';
    }
}
```

On each change in value of the property readyState, the callback function checks for the condition readyState == 4. Whenever this condition
fails to be met, the else condition of the outer loop uses the innerHTML
property to ensure that the page element with id waiting (our <div> element) contains an image whose source is the animated GIF. As soon as
the condition readyState == 4 is met, and we therefore know that the
server request has concluded, the line

```
document.getElementById('waiting').innerHTML = '';
```

once more erases the animation.

We'll see this technique in action in Lesson 11, "Our First Ajax
Application," when we create a complete Ajax application.

Summary

This lesson examined the last link in the Ajax chain: how to deal with
server responses containing both text and XML information.

We also introduced a further JavaScript DOM method,
getElementsByTagName().

In the next lesson, the last in Part II, we use this knowledge along with
that gained from earlier lessons, to construct a complete and working Ajax
application.

LESSON 11

Our First Ajax Application

In this lesson you will learn how to construct a complete and working Ajax application using the techniques discussed in previous lessons.

Constructing the Ajax Application

The previous lessons have introduced all the techniques involved in the design and coding of a complete Ajax application. In this lesson, we're going to construct just such an application.

Our first application will be simple in function, merely returning and displaying the time as read from the server's internal clock; nevertheless it will involve all the basic steps required for any Ajax application:

- An HTML document forming the basis for the application

- JavaScript routines to create an instance of the XMLHTTPRequest object and construct and send asynchronous server calls

- A server-side routine (in PHP) to configure and return the required information

- A callback function to deal with the returned data and use it in the application

Let's get to it, starting with the HTML file that forms the foundation for our application.

The HTML Document

Listing 11.1 shows the code for our HTML page.

LISTING 11.1 The HTML Page for Our Ajax Application

```
<!DOCTYPE HTML PUBLIC "-//W3C//DTD HTML 4.01
➥Transitional//EN"
➥"http://www.w3.org/TR/html4/loose.dtd">
<html>
<head>
<title>Ajax Demonstration</title>
<style>
.displaybox {
width:150px;
background-color:#ffffff;
border:2px solid #000000;
padding:10px;
font:24px normal verdana, helvetica, arial, sans-serif;
}
</style>
</head>
<body style="background-color:#cccccc;
➥text-align:center">

<h1>Ajax Demonstration</h1>
<h2>Getting the server time without page refresh</h2>
<form>
<input type="button" value="Get Server Time" />
</form>
<div id="showtime" class="displaybox"></div>

</body>
</html>
```

This is a simple HTML layout, having only a title, subtitle, button, and
<div> element, plus some style definitions.

> **Tip** In HTML the <div> … </div> element stands for
> division and can be used to allow a number of page
> elements to be grouped together and manipulated in
> a block.

Figure 11.1 shows what the HTML page looks like.

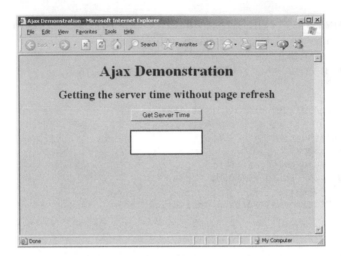

FIGURE 11.1   The HTML file of Listing 11.1.

Adding JavaScript

We can now add our JavaScript routines to the HTML page. We'll do so by adding them inside a `<script>` … `</script>` container to the `<head>` section of the page.

> **Tip**   Alternatively we could have added the routines in an external JavaScript file (ajax.js, say) and called this file from our document by using a statement like:
>
> `<script language="JavaScript" type="text/javascript"`
> `➥src="ajax.js"></script>`
>
> in the `<head>` section of the document.

The XMLHTTPRequest Object

First, let's add our function to create our XMLHTTPRequest object:

```
function getXMLHTTPRequest() {
try {
req = new XMLHttpRequest();
} catch(err1) {
  try {
  req = new ActiveXObject("Msxml2.XMLHTTP");
  } catch (err2) {
    try {
    req = new ActiveXObject("Microsoft.XMLHTTP");
    } catch (err3) {
      req = false;
    }
  }
}
return req;
}
```

It's now a simple matter to create our XMLHTTPRequest object, which on this occasion we're going to call http:

```
var http = getXMLHTTPRequest();
```

The Server Request

Now we need a function to construct our server request, define a callback function, and send the request to the server. This is the function that will be called from an event handler in the HTML page:

```
function getServerTime() {
  var myurl = 'telltimeXML.php';
  myRand = parseInt(Math.random()*999999999999999);
  // add random number to URL to avoid cache problems
  var modurl = myurl+"?rand="+myRand;
  http.open("GET", modurl, true);
  // set up the callback function
  http.onreadystatechange = useHttpResponse;
  http.send(null);
}
```

Once again we have added a parameter with a random value to the URL to avoid any cache problems. Our callback function is named useHttpResponse and is called each time a change is detected in the value of http's readyState property.

Our PHP Server-Side Script

Before explaining the operation of the callback function, we need to refer to the code of the simple PHP server routine telltimeXML.php, shown in Listing 11.2.

LISTING 11.2   telltimeXML.php

```php
<?php
header('Content-Type: text/xml');
echo "<?xml version=\"1.0\" ?><clock1><timenow>"
.date('H:i:s')."</timenow></clock1>";
?>
```

This short program reports the server time using PHP's date() function. The argument passed to this function defines how the elements of the date and time should be formatted. Here we've ignored the date-related elements completely and asked for the time to be returned as Hours:Minutes:Seconds using the 24-hour clock.

Our server script returns an XML file in the following format:

```
<?xml version="1.0" ?>
<clock1>
    <timenow>
    XX:XX:XX
    </timenow>
</clock1>
```

with XX:XX:XX replaced by the current server time. We will use the callback function to extract this time information and display it in the <div> container of the HTML page.

The Callback Function

Here is the code for the callback function useHttpResponse:

```
function useHttpResponse() {
    if (http.readyState == 4) {
     if(http.status == 200) {
        var timeValue = http.responseXML
.getElementsByTagName("timenow")[0];
        document.getElementById('showtime').innerHTML
 = timeValue.childNodes[0].nodeValue;
```

```
  }
} else {
document.getElementById('showtime').innerHTML
= '<img src="anim.gif">';
  }
}
```

Once again we have used the `getElementsByTagname` method, this time to select the `<timenow>` element of the XML data, which we have stored in a variable `timeValue`. However, on this occasion we're not going to display the value in an alert dialog as we did in Lesson 10, "Using the Returned Data."

This time we want instead to use the information to update the contents of an element in the HTML page. Note from Listing 11.1 how the `<div>` container is defined in our HTML page:

```
<div id="showtime" class="displaybox"></div>
```

In addition to the `class` declaration (which is used in the `<style>` definitions to affect how the `<div>` element is displayed), we see that there is also defined an `id` (identity) for the container, with a value set to `showtime`.

Currently the `<div>` contains nothing. We want to update the content of this container to show the server time information stored in `timeValue`. We do so by selecting the page element using JavaScript's `getElementById()` method, which we met in Lesson 10. We'll then use the JavaScript `innerHTML` property to update the element's contents:

```
document.getElementById('showtime').innerHTML
= timeValue.childNodes[0].nodeValue;
```

Employing Event Handlers

Finally, we must decide how the server requests will be triggered. In this case we shall slightly edit the HTML document to use the `onClick()` event handler of the `<button>` object:

```
<input type="button" value="Get Server Time"
onClick="getServerTime()">
```

This will correctly deal with the occasion when the Get Server Time button is clicked. It does, however, leave the <div> element empty when we first load the page.

To overcome this little problem, we can use the onLoad() event handler of the page's <body> element:

```
<body style="background-color:#cccccc"
➥ onLoad="getServerTime()">
```

This event handler fires as soon as the <body> area of the page has finished loading.

Putting It All Together

Listing 11.3 shows the complete client-side code for our Ajax application.

LISTING 11.3   The Complete Ajax Application

```
<html>
<head>
<title>Ajax Demonstration</title>
<style>
.displaybox {
width:150px;
background-color:#ffffff;
border:2px solid #000000;
padding:10px;
font:24px normal verdana, helvetica, arial, sans-serif;
}
</style>
<script language="JavaScript" type="text/javascript">
function getXMLHTTPRequest() {
try {
req = new XMLHttpRequest();
} catch(err1) {
  try {
  req = new ActiveXObject("Msxml2.XMLHTTP");
  } catch (err2) {
    try {
    req = new ActiveXObject("Microsoft.XMLHTTP");
    } catch (err3) {
      req = false;
    }
```

```
      }
   }
   return req;
}

var http = getXMLHTTPRequest();

function getServerTime() {
   var myurl = 'telltimeXML.php';
   myRand = parseInt(Math.random()*999999999999999);
   var modurl = myurl+"?rand="+myRand;
   http.open("GET", modurl, true);
   http.onreadystatechange = useHttpResponse;
   http.send(null);
}

function useHttpResponse() {
    if (http.readyState == 4) {
     if(http.status == 200) {
        var timeValue - http.responseXML
.getElementsByTagName("timenow")[0];
        document.getElementById('showtime').innerHTML
 = timeValue.childNodes[0].nodeValue;
     }
   } else {
   document.getElementById('showtime').innerHTML
 = '<img src="anim.gif">';
   }
}
</script>
</head>
<body style="background-color:#cccccc"
 onLoad="getServerTime()">
<center>
<h1>Ajax Demonstration</h1>
<h2>Getting the server time without page refresh</h2>
<form>
<input type="button" value="Get Server Time"
 onClick="getServerTime()">
</form>
<div id="showtime" class="displaybox"></div>
</center>
</body>
</html>
```

Loading the page into our browser, we can see that the server time is displayed in the <div> container, indicating that the onLoad event handler for the <body> of the page has fired when the page has loaded.

User Feedback

Note also that we have provided user feedback via the line

```
document.getElementById('showtime').innerHTML
➥ = '<img src="anim.gif">';
```

which executes on each change to the value readyState until the condition

```
readyState == 4
```

is satisfied. This line loads into the time display element an animated GIF with a rotating pattern, indicating that a server request is in progress, as shown in Figure 11.2. This technique was described in more detail in Lesson 10.

> **Tip** If you have a fast server and a good Internet connection, it may be difficult to see this user feedback in action because the time display is updated virtually instantaneously. To demonstrate the operation of the animated GIF image, we can slow down the server script to simulate the performance of a more complex script and/or an inferior connection, by using PHP's sleep() command:
>
> ```
> <?php
> header('Content-Type: text/xml');
> sleep(3);
> echo "<?xml version=\"1.0\" ?><clock1><timenow>"
> ➥.date('H:i:s')."</timenow></clock1>";
> ?>
> ```
>
> The line
>
> ```
> sleep(x);
> ```
>
> Forces the server to pause program execution for *x* seconds.

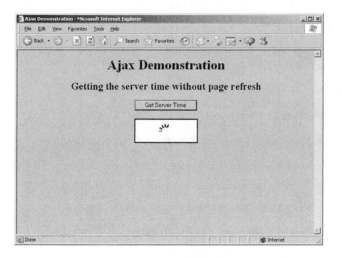

FIGURE 11.2   An animated image provides user feedback.

Now, each time we click on the Get Server Time button, the time display is updated. Figure 11.3 shows the completed application.

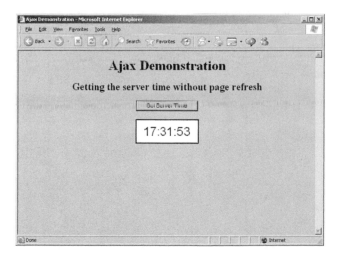

FIGURE 11.3   Our completed Ajax application.

Summary

In this lesson, we constructed a simple yet complete Ajax application that does the following:

- Creates an instance of the XMLHTTPRequest object
- Reacts to JavaScript event handlers built into an HTML page
- Constructs and sends asynchronous server requests
- Parses XML received from the server using JavaScript DOM methods
- Provides user feedback that a request is in progress
- Updates the displayed page with the received data

This completes Part II of the book. Part III, "More Complex Ajax Technologies," investigates some more advanced Ajax techniques.

LESSON 12
Returning Data as Text

In this lesson you will learn some more techniques for using the responseText *property to add functionality to Ajax applications.*

Getting More from the `responseText` Property

The lessons of Part II, "Introducing Ajax," discussed the individual components that make Ajax work, culminating in a complete Ajax application. In Part III, "More Complex Ajax Technologies," each lesson examines how you can extend what you know to develop more sophisticated Ajax applications.

For this lesson, we'll look a little more closely at the responseText property of the XMLHTTPRequest object and see how we can give our application some extra functionality via its use.

As you have seen in previous lessons, the XMLHTTPRequest object provides two properties that contain information received from the server, namely responseText and responseXML. The former presents the calling application with the server data in string format, whereas the latter provides DOM-compatible XML that can be parsed using JavaScript methods.

Although the responseXML property allows you to carry out some sophisticated programming tasks, much can be achieved just by manipulating the value stored in the responseText property.

Returning Text

The term *text* is perhaps a little misleading. The responseText property contains a character string, the value of which you can assign to a JavaScript variable via a simple assignment statement:

```
var mytext = http.responseText;
```

There is no rule saying that the value contained in such a string must be legible text; in fact, the value can contain complete gibberish provided that the string contains only characters that JavaScript accepts in a string variable.

This fact allows a degree of flexibility in what sorts of information you can transfer using this property.

Using Returned Text Directly in Page Elements

Perhaps the simplest example is to consider the use of the value held in responseText in updating the textual part of a page element, say a <div> container. In this case you may simply take the returned string and apply it to the page element in question.

Here's a simple example. The following is the HTML code for an HTML page that forms the basis for an Ajax application:

```
<html>
<head>
  <title>My Ajax Application</title>
</head>
<body>
Here is the text returned by the server:<br />
<div id="myPageElement"></div>
</body>
</html>
```

Clearly this is a simple page that, as it stands, would merely output the line "Here is the text returned by the server:" and nothing else.

Now suppose that we add to the page the necessary JavaScript routines to generate an instance of a XMLHTTPRequest object (in this case called http) and make a server request in response to the onLoad() event handler of the page's <body> Element. Listing 12.1 shows the source code for the revised page.

LISTING 12.1 A Basic Ajax Application Using the responseText Property

```
<html>
<head>
<title>My Ajax Application</title>
<script Language="JavaScript">
function getXMLHTTPRequest() {
```

```
try {
req = new XMLHttpRequest();
} catch(err1) {
  try {
  req = new ActiveXObject("Msxml2.XMLHTTP");
  } catch (err2) {
    try {
    req = new ActiveXObject("Microsoft.XMLHTTP");
    } catch (err3) {
      req = false;
    }
  }
}
return req;
}

var http = getXMLHTTPRequest();

function getServerText() {
  var myurl = 'textserver.php';
  myRand = parseInt(Math.random()*999999999999999);
  var modurl = myurl+"?rand="+myRand;
  http.open("GET", modurl, true);
  http.onreadystatechange = useHttpResponse;
  http.send(null);
}

function useHttpResponse() {
   if (http.readyState == 4) {
    if(http.status == 200) {
       var mytext = http.responseText;
       document.getElementById('myPageElement')
➥.innerHTML = mytext;
    }
  } else {
  document. getElementById('myPageElement')
➥.innerHTML = "";
  }
}

</script>
</head>
<body onLoad="getServerText()">
Here is the text returned by the server:<br>
<div id="myPageElement"></div>
</body>
</html>
```

Most, and probably all, of this code will be familiar from previous lessons. The part that interests us here is the callback function useHttpResponse(), which contains these lines:

```
var mytext = http.responseText;
document.getElementById('myPageElement').innerHTML = mytext;
```

Here we have simply assigned the value received in responseText to become the content of our chosen <div> container.

Running the preceding code with the simple server-side script

```
<?php
echo "This is the text from the server";
?>
```

produces the screen display of Figure 12.1.

FIGURE **12.1**   Displaying text in a page element via responseText.

Including HTML in **responseText**

Now let's modify the code from the preceding example.

As you know from previous lessons, HTML markup is entirely composed of tags written using text characters. If the value contained in the `responseText` property is to be used for modifying the display of the page from which the server request is being sent, there is nothing to stop us having our server script include HTML markup in the information it returns.

Suppose that we once again use the code of Listing 12.1 but with a modified server script:

```php
<?php
echo "<h3>Returning Formatted Text</h3>";
echo "<hr />";
echo "We can use HTML to <strong>format</strong>
➥ text before we return it!";
?>
```

Figure 12.2 shows the resulting browser display.

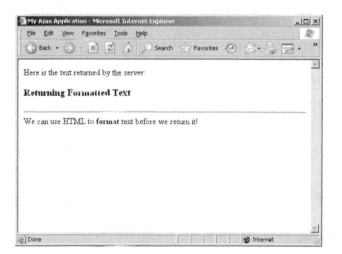

FIGURE 12.2 Display showing HTML formatted at the server.

As a slightly more involved example, consider the case where the server script generates more complex output. We want our application to take this server output and display it as the contents of a table.

This time we'll use our server-side PHP script to generate some tabular information:

```php
<?php
$days = array('Monday','Tuesday','Wednesday',
➥'Thursday','Friday','Saturday','Sunday');
echo "<table border='2'>";
echo "<tr><th>Day Number</th><th>Day Name</th></tr>";
for($i=0;$i<7;$i++)
{
   echo "<tr><td>".$i."</td><td>".$days[$i]."</td></tr>";
}
echo "</table>";
?>
```

Once again using the code of Listing 12.1 to call the server-side script via
XMLHTTPRequest, we obtain a page as displayed in Figure 12.3.

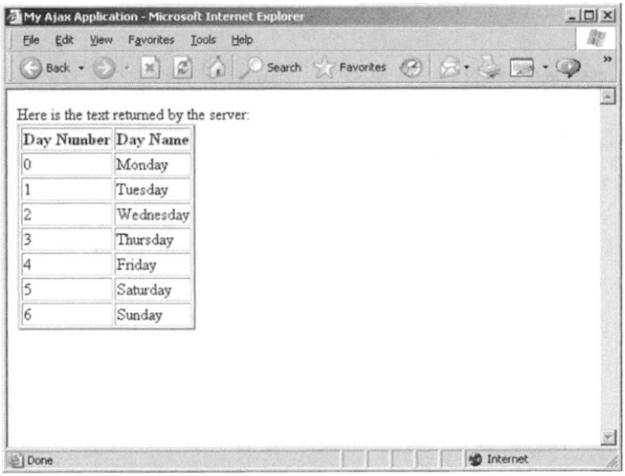

FIGURE **12.3**   Returning more complex HTML.

More Complex Formatted Data

So far we have demonstrated ways to return text that may be directly
applied to an element on a web page. So far, so good. However, if you are
willing to do a little more work in JavaScript to manipulate the returned
data, you can achieve even more.

Provided that the server returns a string value in the responseText property of the XMLHTTPRequest object, you can use any data format you may devise to encode information within it.

Consider the following server-side script, which uses the same data array as in the previous example:

```php
<?php
$days = array('Monday','Tuesday','Wednesday',
➥'Thursday','Friday','Saturday','Sunday');
$numdays = sizeof($days);
for($i=0;$i<($numdays - 1);$i++)
{
echo $days[$i]."¦";
}
echo $days[$numdays-1];
?>
```

> **Note** Note the use of the PHP sizeof() function to determine the number of items in the array. In PHP, as in JavaScript, array keys are numbered from 0 rather than 1.

The string returned in the responseText property now contains the days of the week, separated   or *delimited*—by the pipe character ¦. If we copy this string into a JavaScript variable mystring,

```javascript
var mystring = http.responseText;
```

we will find that the variable mystring contains the string

```
Monday¦Tuesday¦Wednesday¦Thursday¦Friday¦Saturday¦Sunday
```

We may now conveniently divide this string into an array using JavaScript's split() method:

```javascript
var results = http.responseText.split("¦");
```

> **Tip** The JavaScript split() method slices up a string, making each cut wherever in the string it locates the character that it has been given as an argument. That character need not be a pipe; popular alternatives are commas or slashes.

We now have a JavaScript array results containing our data:

```
results[0] = 'Monday'
results[1] = 'Tuesday'
etc…
```

Rather than simply displaying the received data, we now can use it in JavaScript routines in any way we want.

> **Tip** For complex data formats, XML may be a better way to receive and handle data from the server. However, it is remarkable how much can be done just by using the responseText property.

Summary

With little effort, the XMLHTTPRequest object's responseText property can be persuaded to do more than simply return some text to display in a web page.

For all but the most complex data formats, it may prove simpler to manipulate responseText than to deal with the added complexity of XML.

In this lesson you saw several examples of this technique, ranging from the simple update of text content within a page element, to the manipulation of more complex data structures.

LESSON 13

AHAH— Asynchronous HTML and HTTP

In this lesson you will learn how to use AHAH (Asynchronous HTML and HTTP) to build Ajax-style applications without using XML.

Introducing AHAH

You saw in Lesson 12, "Returning Data as Text," just how much can be achieved with an Ajax application without using any XML at all. Many tasks, from simply updating the text on a page to dealing with complicated data structures, can be carried out using only the text string whose value is returned in the XMLHTTPRequest object's responseText property.

It is possible to build complete and useful applications without any XML at all. In fact, the term *AHAH (Asynchronous HTML and HTTP)* has been coined for just such applications.

This lesson takes the concepts of Lesson 12 a little further, examining in more detail where—and how—AHAH can be applied.

> **Note** This technique, a kind of subset of Ajax, has been given various acronyms. These include AHAH (asynchronous HTML and HTTP), JAH (Just Asynchronous HTML), and HAJ (HTML And JavaScript). In this book we'll refer to it as AHAH.

Why Use AHAH Instead of Ajax?

There is no doubt that XML is an important technology with diverse and powerful capabilities. For complex Ajax applications with sophisticated data structures it may well be the best—or perhaps the only—option. However, using XML can sometimes complicate the design of an application, including:

- Work involved in the design of custom schemas for XML data.

- Cross-browser compatibility issues when using JavaScript's DOM methods.

- Performance may suffer from having to carry out processor-intensive XML parsing.

Using AHAH can help you avoid these headaches, while offering a few more advantages too:

- Easy reworking of some preexisting web pages.

- HTML can be easier to fault-find than XML.

- Use of CSS to style the returned information, rather than having to use XSLT.

 Note *XSLT* is a transformation language used to convert XML documents into other formats—for example, into HTML suitable for a browser to display.

In the following sections we'll package our AHAH scripts into a neat external JavaScript file that we can call from our applications.

Creating a Small Library for AHAH

The Ajax applications examined in the last couple of lessons, although complete and functional, involved embedding a lot of JavaScript code into our pages. As you have seen, each application tends to contain similar functions:

- A method to create an instance of the XMLHTTPRequest object, configure it, and send it

- A callback function to deal with the returned text contained in the responseText property

You can abstract these functions into simple JavaScript function calls, especially in cases where you simply want to update a single page element with a new value returned from the server.

Introducing myAHAHlib.js

Consider Listing 13.1; most of this code will be instantly recognizable to you.

LISTING 13.1   myAHAHlib.js

```
function callAHAH(url, pageElement, callMessage) {
     document.getElementById(pageElement)
➥.innerHTML = callMessage;
     try {
     req = new XMLHttpRequest(); /* e.g. Firefox */
     } catch(e) {
       try {
       req = new ActiveXObject("Msxml2.XMLHTTP");
  /* some versions IE */
       } catch (e) {
         try {
         req = new ActiveXObject("Microsoft.XMLHTTP");
  /* some versions IE */
         } catch (E) {
          req = false;
          }
        }
     }
     req.onreadystatechange
➥ = function() {responseAHAH(pageElement);};
     req.open("GET",url,true);
     req.send(null);
  }

function responseAHAH(pageElement) {
   var output = '';
```

continues

LISTING 13.1 Continued

```
  if(req.readyState == 4) {
      if(req.status == 200) {
          output = req.responseText;
          document.getElementById(pageElement)
➥.innerHTML = output;
          }
      }
  }
```

The function `callAHAH()` encapsulates the tasks of creating an instance of the `XMLHTTPRequest` object, declaring the callback function, and sending the request.

Note that instead of simply declaring

```
req.onreadystatechange = responseAHAH;
```

we instead used the JavaScript construct

```
req.onreadystatechange
➥ = function() {responseAHAH(pageElement);};
```

This type of declaration allows us to pass an argument to the declared function, in this case identifying the page element to be updated.

`callAHAH()` also accepts an additional argument, `callMessage`. This argument contains a string defining the content that should be displayed in the target element while we await the outcome of the server request. This provides a degree of feedback for the user, indicating that something is happening on the page. In practice this may be a line of text, such as

```
'Updating page; please wait a moment ….'
```

Once again, however, you may choose to embed some HTML code into this string. Using an animated GIF image within an `<img>` element provides an effective way of warning a user that a process is underway.

The callback function `responseAHAH()` carries out the specific task of applying the string returned in the `responseText` property to the `innerHTML` property of the selected page element `pageElement`:

```
output = req.responseText;
document.getElementById(pageElement).innerHTML = output;
```

This code has been packaged into a file named myAHAHlib.js, which you can call from an HTML page, thus making the functions available to your AHAH application. The next section shows some examples of its use.

Using myAHAHlib.js

In Lesson 4, "Client-Side Coding Using JavaScript," we encountered the concept of JavaScript functions being located in an external file that is referred to within our page.

That's how we'll use our new file myAHAHlib.js, using a statement in this form:

```
<SCRIPT language="JavaScript" SRC="myAHAHlib.js"></SCRIPT>
```

We will then be at liberty to call the functions within the script whenever we want.

The following is the skeleton source code of such an HTML page:

```
<html>
<head>
<title>Another Ajax Application</title>
<SCRIPT language="JavaScript" SRC="myAHAHlib.js"></SCRIPT>
</head>
<body>
<form>
<input type="button" onClick=
➥"callAHAH('serverscript.php?parameter=x',
➥'displaydiv', 'Please wait - page updating …')" >
This is the place where the server response
will be posted:<br>
<div id="displaydiv"></div>
</form>
</body>
</html>
```

In this simple HTML page, a button element is used to create the event that causes the callAHAH() method to be called. This method places the text string

```
'Please wait - page updating …'
```

in the <div> element having id displaydiv and sends the asynchronous server call to the URL serverscript.php?parameter=x.

When responseAHAH() detects that the server has completed its response, the <div> element's content is updated using the value stored in responseText; instead of showing the "please wait" message, the <div> now displays whatever text the server has returned.

Applying myAHAHlib.js in a Project

We can demonstrate these techniques with a further simple Ajax application. This time, we'll build a script to grab the 'keywords' metatag information from a user-entered URL.

> **Note** *Metatags* are optional HTML container elements in the <head> section of an HTML page. They contain data about the web page that is useful to search engines and indexes in deciding how the page's content should be classified. The 'keywords' metatag, where present, typically contains a comma-separated list of words with meanings relevant to the site content. An example of a 'keywords' metatag might look like this:
>
> ```
> <meta name="keywords" content="programming, design,
> ➥ development, Ajax, JavaScript, XMLHTTPRequest,
> ➥script">
> ```

Listing 13.2 shows the HTML code.

LISTING 13.2   getkeywords.html

```
<html>
<head>
<title>A 'Keywords' Metatag Grabber</title>
<SCRIPT language="JavaScript" SRC="myAHAHlib.js">
</SCRIPT>
</head>
<body>
```

```
<script type="text/javascript" src="ahahLib.js">
</script>
<form>
<table>
<tr>
  <td>
    URL: http://
  </td>

  <td>
    <input type="text" id="myurl" name="myurl" size=30>
    <input type="button" onclick =
➥"callAHAH('keywords.php?url='+document
➥.getElementById('myurl').value,'displaydiv',
➥ 'Please wait; loading content …')" value="Fetch">
  </td>
</tr>
<tr><td colspan=2 height=50 id="displaydiv"></td></tr>
</table>
</form>
</body>
</html>
```

Finally, consider the server-side script:

```
<?php
$tags = @get_meta_tags('http://'.$url);
$result = $tags['keywords'];
if(strlen($result) > 0)
{
    echo $result;
} else {
    echo "No keywords metatag is available";
}
?>
```

We present the selected URL to the PHP method get_meta_tags() as an argument:

```
$tags = @get_meta_tags('http://'.$url);
```

This method is specifically designed to parse the metatag information from HTML pages in the form of an associative array. In this script, the array is given the name $tags, and we can recover the 'keywords' metatag by examining the array entry $tags['keywords']; we can then check for the presence or absence of a 'keywords' metatag by measuring the length of the returned string using PHP's strlen() method.

> Tip   The @ character placed before a PHP method tells the PHP interpreter not to output an error message if the method should encounter a problem during execution. We require it in this instance because not all web pages contain a 'keywords' metatag; in the cases where none exists, we would prefer the method to return an empty string so that we can add our own error handling.

When the file getkeywords.html is first loaded into the browser, we are presented with the display shown in Figure 13.1.

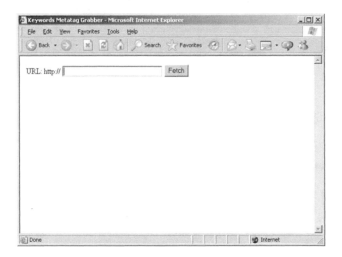

FIGURE 13.1   The browser display after first loading the application.

Here we are invited to enter a URL. When we then click on the Fetch button, callAHAH() is executed and sends our chosen URL as a parameter to the server-side script. At the same time, the message "Please wait; loading content … " is placed in the <div> container. Although possibly only visible for a fraction of a second, we now have a display such as that shown in Figure 13.2.

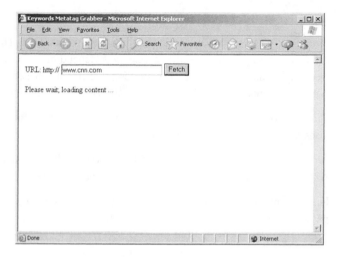

FIGURE 13.2   Awaiting the server response.

Finally, when the server call has concluded, the contents of the responseText property are loaded into the <div> container, producing the display of Figure 13.3.

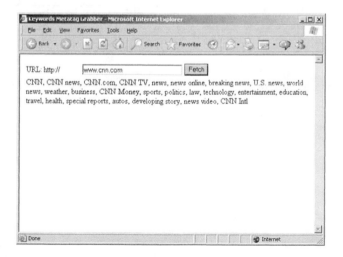

FIGURE 13.3   The keywords are successfully returned.

Extending myAHAHlib.js

As it stands, myAHAHlib.js is a simple implementation of AHAH. There are many ways it could be improved and extended, depending on how it is to be used. Rather than cover these in this lesson, we'll leave these for your own experimentation. Here's a few suggestions to get you started:

- Currently only GET requests are supported. How might the functions be modified to allow POST requests too?

- Much of the user feedback discussed in Lesson 11, "Our First Ajax Application," is not yet implemented in responseAHAH().

- Is it possible for callAHAH() to be modified to accept an array of page elements for updating and (with the aid of a suitable server-side script) process them all at once?

Tip   One option we haven't yet considered is the idea of passing back JavaScript code within responseText. Because JavaScript source code (like everything else in an HTML page) is made up of statements written in plain text, you can return JavaScript source from the server in the responseText property.

You can then execute this JavaScript code using JavaScript's eval() method:

```
eval(object.responseText);
```

Consider the situation where your server script returns the string:

```
"alert('Hello World!');"
```

In this case the eval() method would execute the content as a JavaScript statement, creating a dialog saying 'Hello World!' with an OK button.

Summary

It will hopefully have become clear, in the course of this lesson and Lesson 12, that Ajax can achieve a lot of functionality without using any XML at all.

By carefully using combinations of client-side coding in JavaScript and server-side scripting in your chosen language, you can create data schemes of high complexity.

In simpler applications, where all you want to do is update the text of page elements, the XMLHTTPRequest object's functionality may be abstracted into a JavaScript function library and called from an HTML page via straightforward methods.

For some tasks, however, you need to leverage the power of XML. We'll look at this subject in Lesson 14, "Returning Data as XML."

LESSON 14

Returning Data as XML

In this lesson you will learn to use XML data returned from the server via the responseXML *property of the* XMLHTTPRequest *object.*

Adding the "x" to Ajax

Lesson 12, "Returning Data as Text," and Lesson 13, "AHAH—Asynchronous HTML and HTTP," dealt at some length with the string value contained in responseText and looked at several techniques for using this information in applications. These examples ranged from simple updates of page element text to applications using more sophisticated data structures encoded into string values that can be stored and transferred in the responseText property.

The *X* in Ajax does, of course, stand for XML, and there are good reasons for using the power of XML in your applications. This is particularly true when you need to use highly structured information and/or perform complex translations between different types of data representation.

As discussed previously, the XMLHTTPRequest object has a further property called responseXML, which can be used to transfer information from the server via XML, rather than in text strings.

You saw in Lesson 11, "Our First Ajax Application," how JavaScript's document object model (DOM) methods can help you process this XML information. This lesson looks at these techniques in a little more detail and hopefully gives you a taste of what Ajax applications can achieve when leveraging the power of XML.

The responseXML Property

Whereas the responseText property of the XMLHTTPRequest object contains a string, responseXML can be treated as if it were an XML document.

> **Caution** You need to make sure that your server presents valid and well-formed XML to be returned via the responseXML property. In situations where XML cannot be correctly parsed by the XMLHTTPRequest object, perhaps due to well-formedness errors or problems with unsupported character encoding, the content of the responseXML is unpredictable and also likely to be different in different browsers.

> **Note** Like the responseText property, the value stored in responseXML is read-only, so you cannot write directly to this property; to manipulate it you must copy the value to another variable:
>
> ```
> var myobject = http.responseXML;
> ```

The complete structure and data contained in the XML document can now be made available by using JavaScript's DOM methods. Later in the lesson we'll demonstrate this with another working Ajax application, but first let's revisit the JavaScript DOM methods and introduce a few new ones.

More JavaScript DOM Methods

You met some of the JavaScript DOM methods, such as getElementById and getElementsByTagName, in previous lessons. In those cases, we were mostly concerned with reading the values of the nodes to write those values into HTML page elements.

This lesson looks at the DOM methods that can be used to actually create elements, thereby changing the structure of the page.

The Document Object Model can be thought of as a treelike structure of nodes. As well as reading the values associated with those nodes, you can create and modify the nodes themselves, thereby changing the structure and content of your document.

To add new elements to a page, you need to first create the elements and then attach them to the appropriate point in your DOM tree. Let's look at a simple example using the following HTML document:

```
<html>
<head>
  <title>Test Document</title>
</head>
<body>
We want to place some text here:<br />
<div id="displaydiv"></div>
</body>
</html>
```

In this example, we want to add the text "Hello World!" to the <div> container in the document body. We'll put our JavaScript routine into a function that we'll call from the body's onLoad() event handler.

First, we'll use the JavaScript DOM method createTextNode() to, well, create a text node:

```
var textnode = createTextNode('Hello World!');
```

We now need to attach textnode to the DOM tree of the document at the appropriate point.

You first learned about child nodes in Lesson 4, "Client-Side Coding Using JavaScript"; hopefully, you recall that nodes in a document are said to have *children* if they contain other document elements. JavaScript has an appendChild() method, which allows us to attach our new text node to the DOM tree by making it a child node of an existing document node.

In this case, we want our text to be inside the <div> container having the id displaydiv:

```
var textnode = document.createTextNode('Hello World!');
document.getElementById('displaydiv').appendChild(textnode);
```

 Note Compare this DOM-based method of writing content to the page with the innerHTML method used in the project in Lesson 11.

Let's look at the complete source of the page, after wrapping up this JavaScript code into a function and adding the onLoad() event handler to execute it:

```
<html>
<head>
 <title>Test Document</title>
 <script Language="JavaScript">
 function hello()
 {
  var textnode = document.createTextNode('Hello World!');
  document.getElementById('displaydiv').appendChild(textnode);
 }
 </script>
</head>
<body onLoad="hello()">
We want to place some text here:<br />
<div id="displaydiv"></div>
</body>
</html>
```

Figure 14.1 shows the browser display after loading this page.

Note If you display the source code of this document in your browser, you won't see the 'Hello World!' text inside the <div> container. The browser builds its DOM representation of the HTML document and then uses that model to display the page. The amendments made by your code are made to the DOM, not to the document itself.

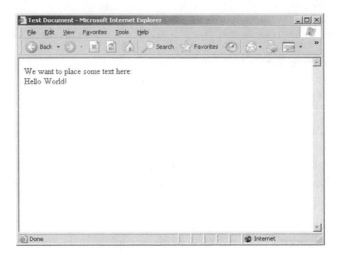

FIGURE 14.1   The DOM says "Hello World!"

When you want to create other page elements besides text nodes, you can do so using the createElement() method, which works pretty much like createTextNode(). We could, in fact, have used createElement() to create the <div> container itself, prior to adding our 'Hello World!' text node:

```
var newdiv = document.createElement("div");
```

In general, you simply pass the type of the required page element as an argument to createElement() to generate the required type of element.

An Overview of DOM Methods

This book is about Ajax, not just about JavaScript DOM techniques, so we're not going to reproduce here a comprehensive guide to all the available methods and properties. However, Table 14.1 itemizes some of the more useful ones.

> **Tip** If you need a more comprehensive account of the JavaScript DOM methods and properties, Andrew Watt gives a useful list in his excellent book *Sams Teach Yourself XML in 10 Minutes* (Sams Publishing, ISBN 0672324717).

TABLE 14.1 Some JavaScript DOM Properties and Methods

Node Properties

childNodes	Array of child nodes
firstChild	The first Child node
lastChild	The last Child node
nodeName	Name of the node
nodeType	Type of node
nodeValue	Value contained in the node
nextSibling	Next node sharing the same parent
previousSibling	Previous node sharing same parent
parentNode	Parent of this node

Node Methods

AppendChild	Add a new child node
HasChildNodes	True if this node has children
RemoveChild	Deletes a child node

Document Methods

CreateAttribute	Make a new attribute for an element
CreateElement	Make a new document element
CreateTextNode	Make a text item
GetElementsByTagName	Create an array of tagnames
GetElementsById	Find an element by its ID

Project—An RSS Headline Reader

Let's now take what we've learned about returning XML data from the server and use these techniques to tackle a new project.

XML data is made available on the Internet in many forms. One of the most popular is the RSS feed, a particular type of XML source usually containing news or other topical and regularly updated items. RSS feeds are available from many sources on the Web, including most broadcast companies and newspaper publishers, as well as specialist sites for all manner of subjects.

We'll write an Ajax application to take a URL for an RSS feed, collect the XML, and list the titles and descriptions of the news items contained in the feed.

The following is part of the XML for a typical RSS feed:

```
<rss version="0.91">
<channel>
<title>myRSSfeed.com</title>
<link>http://www.********.com/</link>
<description>My RSS feed</description>
<language>en-us</language>
<item>
<title>New Store Opens</title>
<link>http://www.**********.html</link>
<description>A new music store opened today in Canal Road.
➥The new business, Ajax Records, caters for a wide range of
➥musical tastes.</description>
</item>
<item>
<title>Bad Weather Affects Transport</title>
<link>http://www.***********.html</link>
<description>Trains and buses were disrupted badly today
➥due to sudden heavy snow.  Police advised people not to
➥travel unless absolutely necessary.</description>
</item>
<item>
<title>Date Announced for Mayoral Election</title>
<link>http://www.*********.html</link>
```

```
<description>September 4th has been announced as the date
➥for the next mayoral election.  Watch local news for more
➥details.</description>
</item>
</channel>
</rss>
```

From the first line

```
<rss version="0.91">
```

we see that we are dealing with RSS version 0.91 in this case. The versions of RSS differ quite a bit, but for the purposes of our example we only care about the `<title>`, `<link>`, and `<description>` elements for the individual news items, which remain essentially unchanged from version to version.

The HTML Page for Our Application

Our page needs to contain an input field for us to enter the URL of the required RSS feed and a button to instruct the application to collect the data. We also will have a `<div>` container in which to display our parsed data:

```
<html>
<head>
<title>An Ajax RSS Headline Reader</title>
</head>
<body>
<h3>An Ajax RSS Reader</h3>
<form name="form1">
URL of RSS feed: <input type="text" name="feed" size="50"
➥value="http://"><input type="button" value="Get Feed">
<br /><br />
<div id="news"><h4>Feed Titles</h4></div>
</form>
</html>
```

If we save this code to a file rss.htm and load it into our browser, we see something like the display shown in Figure 14.2.

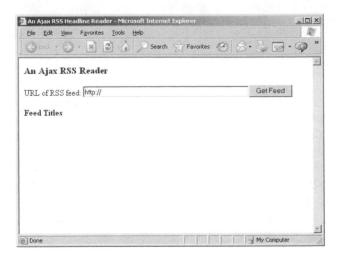

FIGURE **14.2**   Displaying the base HTML document for our RSS headline reader.

Much of the code for our reader will be familiar by now; the means of creating an instance of the XMLHTTPRequest object, constructing and sending a server request, and checking when that request has been completed are all carried out much as in previous examples.

This time, however, instead of using responseText we will be receiving data in XML via the responseXML property. We'll use that data to modify the DOM of our HTML page to show the news items' titles and descriptions in a list within the page's <div> container. Each title and description will be contained in its own paragraph element (which we'll also construct for the purpose) and be styled via a style sheet to display as we want.

The Code in Full

Let's jump right in and look at the code, shown in Listing 14.1.

LISTING 14.1   Ajax RSS Headline Reader

```
<html>
<head>
<title>An Ajax RSS Headline Reader</title>
</head>
<style>
```

```css
.title {
font: 16px bold helvetica, arial, sans-serif;
padding: 0px 30px 0px 30px;
text-decoration:underline;
}
.descrip {
font: 14px normal helvetica, arial, sans-serif;
text-decoration:italic;
padding: 0px 30px 0px 30px;
background-color:#cccccc;
}
.link {
font: 9px bold helvetica, arial, sans-serif;
padding: 0px 30px 0px 30px;
}
.displaybox {
border: 1px solid black;
padding: 0px 50px 0px 50px;
}
</style>
<script language="JavaScript" type="text/javascript">
function getXMLHTTPRequest() {
try {
req = new XMLHttpRequest(); /* e.g. Firefox */
} catch(e) {
  try {
  req = new ActiveXObject("Msxml2.XMLHTTP");
  /* some versions IE */
  } catch (e) {
    try {
    req = new ActiveXObject("Microsoft.XMLHTTP");
    /* some versions IE */
    } catch (E) {
      req = false;
    }
  }
}
return req;
}

var http = getXMLHTTPRequest();

function getRSS() {
  var myurl = 'rssproxy.php?feed=';
  var myfeed = document.form1.feed.value;
    myRand = parseInt(Math.random()*999999999999999);
    // cache buster
```

continues

LISTING 14.1   Continued

```
    var modurl = myurl+escape(myfeed)+"&rand="+myRand;
    http.open("GET", modurl, true);
    http.onreadystatechange = useHttpResponse;
    http.send(null);
}

function useHttpResponse() {
   if (http.readyState == 4) {
     if(http.status == 200) {
         // first remove the childnodes
         // presently in the DM
         while (document.getElementById('news')
➥.hasChildNodes())
         {
document.getElementById('news').removeChild(document
➥.getElementById('news').firstChild);
         }
         var titleNodes = http.responseXML
➥.getElementsByTagName("title");
         var descriptionNodes = http.responseXML
➥.getElementsByTagName("description");
         var linkNodes = http.responseXML
➥.getElementsByTagName("link");
         for(var i =1;i<titleNodes.length;i++)
         {
            var newtext = document
➥.createTextNode(titleNodes[i]
➥.childNodes[0].nodeValue);
            var newpara = document.createElement('p');
            var para = document.getElementById('news')
➥.appendChild(newpara);
            newpara.appendChild(newtext);
            newpara.className = "title";

            var newtext2 = document
➥.createTextNode(descriptionNodes[i]
➥.childNodes[0].nodeValue);
            var newpara2 = document.createElement('p');
            var para2 = document
➥.getElementById('news').appendChild(newpara2);
            newpara2.appendChild(newtext2);
            newpara2.className = "descrip";
            var newtext3 = document
➥.createTextNode(linkNodes [i]
➥.childNodes[0].nodeValue);
            var newpara3 = document.createElement('p');
```

```
            var para3 = document.getElementById('news')
➥.appendChild(newpara3);
            newpara3.appendChild(newtext3);
            newpara3.className = "link";
          }
        }
      }
}
</script>
<body>
<center>
<h3>An Ajax RSS Reader</h3>
<form name="form1">
URL of RSS feed: <input type="text" name="feed"
➥size="50" value="http://"><input type="button"
➥onClick="getRSS()" value="Get Feed"><br><br>
<div id="news" class="displaybox">
➥<h4>Feed Titles</h4></div>
</form>
</center>
</html>
```

Mostly we are concerned with describing the workings of the callback function `useHttpResponse()`.

The Callback Function

In addition to the usual duties of checking the XMLHTTPRequest readyState and status properties, this function undertakes for us the following tasks:

- Remove from the display <div> any display elements from previous RSS listings.

- Parse the incoming XML to extract the title, link, and description elements.

- Construct DOM elements to hold and display these results.

- Apply CSS styles to these elements to change how they are displayed in the browser.

To remove the DOM elements installed by previous news imports (where they exist), we first identify the <div> element by using its ID and then use the hasChildNodes() DOM method, looping through and deleting the first child node from the <div> element each time until none remain:

```
while (document.getElementById('news').hasChildNodes())
{
document.getElementById('news')
➥.removeChild(document.getElementById('news').firstChild);
}
```

The following explanation describes the processing of the title elements, but, as can be seen from Listing 14.1, we repeat the process identically to retrieve the description and link information too.

To parse the XML content to extract the item titles, we build an array `titleNodes` from the XML data stored in `responseXML`:

```
var titleNodes
➥ = http.responseXML.getElementsByTagName("title");
```

We can then loop through these items, processing each in turn:

```
for(var i =1;i<titleNodes.length;i++)
        { … processing instructions … }
```

For each title, we need to first extract the title text using the `nodeValue` property:

```
var newtext = document.createTextNode(titleNodes[i]
➥.childNodes[0].nodeValue);
```

We can then create a paragraph element:

```
var newpara = document.createElement('p');
```

append the paragraph as a child node of the `<div>` element:

```
var para = document.getElementById('news')
➥.appendChild(newpara);
```

and apply the text content to the paragraph element:

```
newpara.appendChild(newtext);
```

Finally, using the `className` property we can define how the paragraph is displayed. The class declarations appear in a `<style>` element in the document head and provide a convenient means of changing the look of the RSS reader to suit our needs.

```
newpara.className = "title";
```

Each time we enter the URL of a different RSS feed into the input field and click the button, the `<div>` content is updated to show the items belonging to the new RSS feed. This being an Ajax application, there is of course no need to reload the whole page.

The Server-Side Code

Because of the security constraints built into the XMLHTTPRequest object, we can't call an RSS feed directly; we must use a script having a URL on our own server, and have this script collect the remote XML file and deliver it to the Ajax application.

In this case, we do not require that the server side script rssproxy.php should *modify* the XML file but simply route it back to us via the responseXML property of the XMLHTTPRequest object. We say that the script is acting as a proxy because it is retrieving the remote resource on behalf of the Ajax application.

Listing 14.2 shows the code of the PHP script.

LISTING 14.2   Server Script for the RSS Headline Reader

```php
<?php
$mysession = curl_init($_GET['feed']);
curl_setopt($mysession, CURLOPT_HEADER, false);
curl_setopt($mysession, CURLOPT_RETURNTRANSFER, true);
$out = curl_exec($mysession);
header("Content-Type: text/xml");
echo $out;
curl_close($mysession);
?>
```

The script uses the cURL PHP library, a set of routines for making Internet file transfer easier to program. A full description of cURL would not be appropriate here; suffice to say that this short script first receives the URL of the required RSS feed by referring to the feed variable sent by the Ajax application. The two lines that call the `curl_setopt()` function declare, respectively, that we don't want the headers sent with the remote file, but we do want the file contents. The `curl_exec()` function then makes the data transfer.

After that it's simply a matter of adding an appropriate header by using the familiar PHP `header()` command and returning the data to our Ajax application.

> **Tip** For a full description of using cURL with PHP, see the PHP website at http://uk2.php.net/curl and/or the cURL site at http://curl.haxx.se/.

Figure 14.3 shows the RSS reader in action, in this case displaying content from a CNN newsfeed.

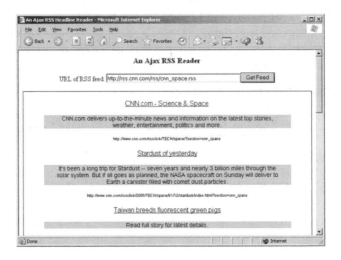

FIGURE 14.3   The Ajax RSS reader in action.

Summary

The JavaScript DOM methods, when used with the `XMLHTTPRequest` object and XML data, provide a powerful means of transferring, organizing, and either displaying or otherwise processing data that has a sophisticated structure.

In this lesson you saw how DOM elements can be added, deleted, and manipulated to restructure an application's DOM in accordance with XML data received in the `XMLHTTPRequest` object's `responseXML` property.

Lesson 15

Web Services and the REST Protocol

In this lesson you will learn the basics of web services and how to implement them using the REST (Representational State Transfer) protocol.

Introduction to Web Services

So far you have seen several example applications in which we have called server-side scripts to carry out tasks. In each case we devised data structures to transfer the information and written routines to handle data transfer both to and from the server.

Suppose, though, that you wanted to make your server-side programs more generally available. Perhaps you can imagine that several different web applications might interface with such scripts for their own purposes. As well as browsers requesting pages directly, perhaps other applications (for example Ajax applications operating via XMLHTTPRequest calls) might also make data requests and expect to receive, in response, data that they can understand and manipulate.

In such cases it would be beneficial to have some form of standardization in the interfaces that your program makes available. This principle provides the basis of what have come to be known as *web services*.

As an example, suppose that our server application produces XML-formatted weather forecast data in response to a request containing geographical information.

The nature of this type of service makes it broadly applicable; such an application might have a wide variety of "clients" ranging from simple web pages that present weather forecasts in their local area to complex aviation or travel planning applications that require the data for more demanding uses.

This type of service is just one small example of what a web service might be capable of doing. Thousands of web services are active on the Internet, providing a mind-boggling array of facilities including user authentication, payment processing, content syndication, messaging, and a host of others.

In general, a web service makes available an application programming interface (API), which allows client applications to build interfaces to the service. Although any Internet protocol might be used to create web services, XML and HTTP are popular options.

A number of protocols and techniques have emerged that help you to create and utilize web services. This lesson looks at perhaps the simplest of those, called *REST* (*Representational State Transfer*), and Lesson 16, "Web Services Using SOAP," discusses another protocol, this time called *SOAP* (the *Simple Object Access Protocol*). Each lesson highlights in particular how they may be useful in Ajax applications.

REST—Representational State Transfer

REST is centered on two main principles for generalized network design:

- Resources are represented by URLs—A resource can be thought of as a "noun" and refers to some entity we want to deal with in the API of a web service; this could be a document, a person, a meeting, a location, and so on. Each resource in a REST application has a unique URL.

- Operations are carried out via standard HTTP methods—HTTP methods such as GET, POST, PUT, and DELETE are used to carry out operations on resources. In this way we can consider such operations as "verbs" acting on resources.

A Hypothetical REST Example

To understand how and why we might apply these ideas, let's look at a hypothetical example.

Suppose that we have a web service that allows writers to submit, edit, and read articles. Applying so-called RESTful principles to the design of this application, the following occurs:

- Each submitted article has a unique URL, for example:

  `http://somedomain.com/articles/173`

  We only require that the URL be unique for each article; for instance

  `http://somedomain.com/articles/list.php?id=173`

  also fulfils this requirement.

> **Tip**   Although REST requires that URLs be unique, it does not follow that each resource must have a corresponding physical page. In many cases the resource is generated by the web service at the time of the request—for example, by reference to a database.

- To retrieve an article to read or edit, our client application would simply use an HTTP `GET` request to the URL of the article in question.

- To upload a new article, a `POST` request would be used, containing information about the article. The server would respond with the URL of the newly uploaded article.

- To upload an edited article, a `PUT` request would be used, containing the revised content.

- HTTP `DELETE` would be employed to delete a particular article.

In this way, the web service is using an interface familiar to anyone who has used the World Wide Web. We do not need to devise a library of API methods for sending or retrieving information; we already have them in the form of the standard HTTP methods.

> ✎ **Note**   The World Wide Web itself is a REST application.

Query Information Using GET

An important issue concerning the use of the HTTP GET request in a RESTful application is that it should never change the server state. To put it another way: We only use GET requests to ask for information from the server, never to add or alter information already there.

POST, PUT, and DELETE calls can all change the server status in some way.

Stateless Operation

All server exchanges within a RESTful application should be *stateless*. By stateless we mean that the call itself must contain all the information required by the server to carry out the required task, rather than depending on some state or context currently present on the server. We cannot, for example, require the server to refer to information sent in previous requests.

Using REST in Practice

Let's expand on the example quoted earlier involving our articles web service.

Reading a List of Available Articles

The list of available articles is a resource. Because the web service conforms to REST principles, we expect the service to provide a URL by which we can access this resource, for instance:

```
http://somedomain.com/articles/list.php
```

Because we are querying information, rather than attempting to change it, we simply use an HTTP GET request to the preceding URL. The server may return, for example, the following XML:

```
<articles>
    <article>
        <id>173</id>
        <title>New Concepts in Ajax</title>
        <author>P.D. Johnstone</author>
    </article>
    <article>
        <id>218</id>
        <title>More Ajax Ideas</title>
        <author>S.N. Braithwaite</author>
    </article>
    <article>
        <id>365</id>
        <title>Pushing the Ajax Envelope</title>
        <author>Z.R. Lawson</author>
    </article>
</articles>
```

Retrieving a Particular Article

Because this is another request for information, we are again required to submit an HTTP GET request. Our web service might perhaps allow us to make a request to

```
http://somedomain.com/articles/list.php?id=218
```

and receive in return

```
<article>
    <id>218</id>
    <title>More Ajax Ideas</title>
    <author>S.N. Braithwaite</author>
</article>
```

Uploading a New Article

In this instance we need to issue a POST request rather than a GET request. In cases similar to the hypothetical one outlined previously, it is likely that the server will assign the id value of a new article, leaving us to encode parameter and value pairs for the title and author elements:

```
var articleTitle = 'Another Angle on Ajax';
var articleAuthor = 'K.B. Schmidt';
var url = '/articles/upload.php';
var poststring = "title="+encodeURI(articleTitle)
➥+"&author="+encodeURI(articleAuthor);
http.onreadystatechange = callbackFunction();
http.open('POST', url, true);
http.setRequestHeader("Content-type",
➥"application/x-www-form-urlencoded");
http.setRequestHeader("Content-length", poststring.length);
http.send(poststring);
```

Real World REST—the Amazon REST API

Leading online bookseller Amazon.com makes available a set of REST
web services to help developers integrate Amazon browsing and shopping
facilities into their web applications.

> **Note**   Amazon.com often refers to the REST protocol
> as *XML-over-HTTP* or *XML/HTTP*.

By first creating a URL containing parameter/value pairs for the required
search parameters (such as publisher, sort order, author, and so on) and
then submitting a GET request to this URL, the Amazon web service can be
persuaded to return an XML document containing product details. We may
then parse that XML to create DOM objects for display in a web page or
to provide data for further processing as required by our application.

> **Tip**   Amazon requires that you obtain a *developer's
> token* to develop client applications for its web ser-
> vices. You will need this token in constructing REST
> requests to Amazon's web services. You can also
> obtain an Amazon Associate's ID to enable you to
> earn money by carrying Amazon services on your web-
> site. See http://www.amazon.com for details.

Let's see this in practice by developing a REST request to return a list of books. Many types of searches are possible, but in this example, we request a list of books published by Sams.

We start to construct the GET request with the base URL:

```
$url = 'http://xml.amazon.com/onca/xml3';
```

We then need to add a number of parameter/value pairs to complete the request:

```
$assoc_id = "XXXXXXXXXX";    // your Amazon Associate's ID
$dev_token = "ZZZZZZZZZZ";    // Your Developer Token
$manuf = "Sams";
$url = "http://xml.amazon.com/onca/xml3";
$url .= "?t=".$assoc_id;
$url .= "&dev-t=".$dev_token;
$url .= "&ManufacturerSearch=".$ manuf;
$url .= "&mode=books";
$url .= "&sort=+salesrank";
$url .= "&offer=All";
$url .="&type=lite";
$url .= "&page=1";
$url .= "&f-xml";
```

Submitting this URL, we receive an XML file containing details of all matching books. I won't reproduce the whole file here (there are more than 5,000 titles!), but Listing 15.1 shows an extract from the XML file, including the first book in the list.

LISTING 15.1 Example of XML Returned by Amazon Web Service

```
<?xml version="1.0" encoding="UTF-8" ?>
 <ProductInfo xmlns:xsi="http://www.w3.org/
➥2001/XMLSchema-instance"
➥ xsi:noNamespaceSchemaLocation
➥="http://xml.amazon.com/schemas3/dev-lite.xsd">
 <Request>
 <Args>
  <Arg value="Mozilla/4.0 (compatible; MSIE 6.0;
➥Windows NT 5.1; SV1; .NET CLR 1.1.4322)"
➥ name="UserAgent" />
  <Arg value="0G2CGCT7MRWB37PXAS4B" name="RequestID" />
  <Arg value="All" name="offer" />
```

continues

LISTING 15.1 Continued

```
<Arg value="us" name="locale" />
<Arg value="1" name="page" />
<Arg value="ZZZZZZZZZZZ" name="dev-t" />
<Arg value="XXXXXXXXXX" name="t" />
<Arg value="xml" name="f" />
<Arg value="books" name="mode" />
<Arg value="Sams" name="ManufacturerSearch" />
<Arg value="lite" name="type" />
<Arg value="salesrank" name="sort" />
</Args>
</Request>
<TotalResults>5051</TotalResults>
<TotalPages>506</TotalPages>
<Details url="http://www.amazon.com/exec/obidos/ASIN/
➥0672327236/themousewhisp-20?dev-t=
➥1WPTTG90FS816BXMNFG2%26camp=2025%26link_code=xm2">
<Asin>0672327236</Asin>
<ProductName>Sams Teach Yourself Microsoft SharePoint
➥2003 in 10 Minutes (Sams Teach Yourself
➥in 10 Minutes)</ProductName>
<Catalog>Book</Catalog>
<Authors>
<Author>Colin Spence</Author>
<Author>Michael Noel</Author>
</Authors>
<ReleaseDate>06 December, 2004</ReleaseDate>
<Manufacturer>Sams</Manufacturer>
<ImageUrlSmall>http://images.amazon.com/images/P/
➥0672327236.01.THUMBZZZ.jpg</ImageUrlSmall>
<ImageUrlMedium>http://images.amazon.com/images/P/
➥0672327236.01.MZZZZZZZ.jpg</ImageUrlMedium>
<ImageUrlLarge>http://images.amazon.com/images/P/
➥0672327236.01.LZZZZZZZ.jpg</ImageUrlLarge>
<Availability>Usually ships in 24 hours</Availability>
<ListPrice>$14.99</ListPrice>
<OurPrice>$10.19</OurPrice>
<UsedPrice>$9.35</UsedPrice>
</Details>
```

Clearly we can now process this XML document in any way we want. For example, Lesson 14, "Returning Data as XML," discussed how to use JavaScript DOM methods to select information from the XML document and place it in page elements added to the DOM of our document.

REST and Ajax

You know already that the XMLHTTPRequest object has methods that allow you to directly deal with HTTP request types and URLs.

Accessing RESTful web services is therefore simplified to a great extent. Because you know that each resource exposed by the web service API has a unique URL, and that the methods made available by the service are standard HTTP methods, it becomes a simple matter to construct the required XMLHTTPRequest calls.

The prospect of being able to access a wide variety of web services from within Ajax applications, and use the returned information within those applications, is attractive—even more so if you can use a consistent and simple interface protocol.

Summary

This lesson introduced the concept of web services and the principles underlying the REST protocol.

REST requires that all resources be made accessible via unique URLs and that all required actions can be carried out on those resources by means of the standard HTTP methods. This makes RESTful web services interface comfortably with Ajax applications, due to the XMLHTTPRequest object having methods that directly reference URLs and HTTP methods to create server requests.

Lesson 16 discusses a different style of web service using SOAP and how it relates to Ajax development.

LESSON 16
Web Services Using SOAP

In this lesson you will learn about using web services with the SOAP protocol.

Introducing SOAP (Simple Object Access Protocol)

In Lesson 15, "Web Services and the REST Protocol," we discussed web services and in particular saw how the REST (Representational State Transfer) protocol can be used to provide a consistent application programming interface (API) to such services.

REST is a good example of a protocol designed to operate with *resource-oriented* services, those that provide a simple mechanism to locate a resource and a set of basic methods that can manipulate that resource. In a resource-oriented service, those methods normally revolve around creating, retrieving, modifying, and deleting pieces of information.

In the case of REST, the methods are those specified in the HTTP specifications—GET, POST, PUT, and DELETE.

In certain cases, however, we are more interested in the *actions* a web service can carry out than in the resources it can control. We might perhaps call such services *action-oriented*. In these situations the resources themselves may have some importance, but the key issues concern the details of the activities undertaken by the service.

Perhaps the most popular and widely used protocol for designing action-oriented web services is SOAP, the Simple Object Access Protocol.

This lesson looks at SOAP, comparing and contrasting it where appropriate with the REST protocol discussed in Lesson 15.

Note The full name Simple Object Access Protocol has been dropped in the later versions of the SOAP specifications, as it was felt that the direction of the project had shifted and the name was no longer appropriate. The protocol continues to be referred to as SOAP.

The Background of the SOAP Protocol

SOAP began in the late 1990s when XML was itself a fledgling web technology and was offered to the W3C in 2000. SOAP and another XML-based web service protocol, called XML-RPC, had a joint upbringing.

SOAP was designed essentially as a means of packaging remote procedure calls (requests to invoke programs on remote machines) into XML wrappers in a standardized way.

Numerous enterprises contributed to the early development of SOAP, including IBM, Microsoft, and Userland. The development of SOAP later passed to the XML Protocols Working Group of the W3C.

Tip You can get the latest information on the SOAP specification from the W3C website at http://www.w3.org/2000/xp/Group/.

The SOAP Protocol

SOAP is an XML-based messaging protocol. A SOAP request is an XML document with the following main constituents:

- An *envelope* that defines the document as a SOAP request

- A body element containing information about the call and the expected responses

- Optional header and fault elements that carry supplementary information

Let's look at a skeleton SOAP request:

```
<?xml version="1.0"?>
<SOAP-ENV:Envelope
xmlns:SOAP-ENV="http://schemas.xmlsoap.org/soap/envelope/"
SOAP-ENV:encodingStyle=
➥"http://schemas.xmlsoap.org/soap/encoding/">
<SOAP-ENV:Header>
  ... various commands . . .
</SOAP-ENV:Header>
<SOAP-ENV:Body>
... various commands . . .
  <SOAP-ENV:Fault>
... various commands . . .
  </SOAP-ENV:Fault>
</SOAP-ENV:Body>
</SOAP-ENV:Envelope>
```

Note that the SOAP request is an XML file, which has as its root the Envelope element.

The first line of the Envelope is

```
<SOAP-ENV:Envelope xmlns:SOAP-EN =
➥"http://schemas.xmlsoap.org/soap/envelope/"
SOAP-ENV:encodingStyle=
➥"http://schemas.xmlsoap.org/soap/encoding/">
```

This line declares the xmlns:soap namespace, which must always have the value xmlns:soap="http://schemas.xmlsoap.org/soap/envelope/".

> **Tip**   A *namespace* is an identifier used to uniquely group a set of XML elements or attributes, providing a means to qualify their names, so that names in other schemas do not conflict with them.

The encodingStyle attribute contains information defining the data types used in the message.

Next appears the Header element, which is optional but must, if present, be the first element in the message. Attributes defined in the Header element define how the message is to be processed by the receiving application.

The body element of the SOAP message contains the message intended for the final recipient.

The serialized method arguments are contained within the SOAP request's body element. The call's XML element must immediately follow the opening XML tag of the SOAP body and must have the same name as the remote method being called.

The body may also contain a Fault element (but no more than one). This element is defined in the SOAP specification and is intended to carry information about any errors that may have occurred. If it exists, it must be a child element of the body element. The Fault element has various child elements including faultcode, faultstring, and detail, which contain specific details of the fault condition.

Code Example of a SOAP Request

Let's see how a typical SOAP request might look:

```
<?xml version="1.0"?>
<SOAP-ENV:Envelope xmlns:SOAP-ENV=
➥"http://schemas.xmlsoap.org/soap/envelope/" SOAP
➥ENV:encodingStyle="http://schemas.xmlsoap.org/
➥soap/encoding/">
<SOAP-ENV:Body>
    <m:GetInvoiceTotal xmlns:m=
➥"http://www.somedomain.com/invoices">
        <m:Invoice>77293</m:Invoice>
    </m:GetInvoiceTotal>
</SOAP-ENV:Body>
</SOAP-ENV:Envelope>
```

In the preceding example, the m:GetInvoiceTotal and m:Invoice elements are specific to the particular application, and are not part of SOAP itself. These elements constitute the message contained in the SOAP envelope.

Let's see what the SOAP response from the web service might look like:

```
<?xml version="1.0"?>
<SOAP-ENV:Envelope xmlns:SOAP-ENV=
➥"http://schemas.xmlsoap.org/soap/envelope/" SOAP
➥ENV:encodingStyle="http://schemas.xmlsoap.org/
➥soap/encoding/">
<SOAP-ENV:Body>
```

```
    <m:ShowInvoiceTotal xmlns:m=
➡"http://www.somedomain.com/invoices">
        <m:InvoiceTotal>3295.00</m:InvoiceTotal>
    </m:ShowInvoiceTotal>
</SOAP-ENV:Body>
</SOAP-ENV:Envelope>
```

Sending the SOAP Request Via HTTP

A SOAP message may be transmitted via HTTP GET or HTTP POST. If
sent via HTTP POST, the SOAP message requires at least one HTTP
header to be set; this defines the Content-Type:

```
Content-Type: text/xml
```

After a successful SOAP exchange, you would expect to receive the
SOAP response preceded by an appropriate HTTP header:

```
HTTP/1.1 200 OK
Content-Type: text/xml
Content-Length: yyy
<?xml version="1.0"?>
<SOAP-ENV:Envelope xmlns:SOAP-ENV=
➡"http://schemas.xmlsoap.org/soap/envelope/" SOAP-
ENV:encodingStyle="http://schemas.xmlsoap.org/soap/encoding/">
<SOAP-ENV:Body>
    <m:ShowInvoiceTotal xmlns:m=
➡"http://www.somedomain.com/invoices">
        <m:InvoiceTotal>3295.00</m:InvoiceTotal>
    </m:ShowInvoiceTotal>
</SOAP-ENV:Body>
</SOAP-ENV:Envelope>
```

Using Ajax and SOAP

To use SOAP with Ajax, you need to perform a number of separate steps:

1. Create the SOAP envelope.

2. Serialize the application-specific information into XML.

3. Create the SOAP body containing a serialized version of your application-specific code.

4. Send an HTTP request via the XMLHTTPRequest object, containing the SOAP message as a payload.

The callback function then needs to be responsible for unpacking the SOAP response and parsing the XML contained inside it.

Code Example

How might the resulting code look? Let's see an example using the fictitious SOAP web service of the previous example:

```
var invoiceno = '77293';
http.open("POST", "http://somedomain.com/invoices",true);
http.onreadystatechange=function()  {
  if (http.readyState==4)   {
    if(http.status==200) {
      alert('The server said: '+ http.responseText)
    }
  }
}
http.setRequestHeader("Content-Type", "text/xml")
var mySOAP = '<?xml version="1.0"?>'
  + '<SOAP-ENV:Envelope xmlns:SOAP-ENV='
➥"http://schemas.xmlsoap.org/soap/envelope/"'
  + ' SOAP-ENV:encodingStyle='
➥"http://schemas.xmlsoap.org/soap/encoding/">'
  + '<SOAP-ENV:Body>'
  + '<m:GetInvoiceTotal xmlns:m='
➥"http://www.somedomain.com/invoices">'
  + '<m:Invoice>'+invoiceno+'</m:Invoice></m:GetInvoiceTotal>'
  + '</SOAP-ENV:Body></SOAP-ENV:Envelope>';
http.send(mySOAP);
```

Here we have constructed the entire SOAP envelope in a JavaScript string variable, before passing it to the send() function of the XMLHTTPRequest object.

The value returned from the server needs to be parsed first to remove the SOAP response wrapper and then to recover the application data from the body section of the SOAP message.

Reviewing SOAP and REST

Over the course of this lesson and Lesson 15, we've looked at the REST and SOAP approaches to using web services.

Although other web services protocols exist, a significant REST versus SOAP argument has been waged among developers over the last couple of years.

I don't intend to join that argument in this book. Instead, let's summarize the similarities and differences between the two approaches:

- REST leverages the standard HTTP methods of PUT, GET, POST, and DELETE to create remote procedure calls having comparable functions. Web service implementations using the REST protocol seem particularly suited toward resource-based services, where the most-used methods generally involve creating, editing, retrieving, and deleting information. On the downside, REST requires a little more knowledge about the HTTP protocol.

- The SOAP protocol adds substantial complexity, with the necessity to serialize the remote call and then construct a SOAP envelope to contain it. Further work arises from the need to "unpack" the returned data from its SOAP envelope before parsing the data. These extra steps can also have an impact on performance, with SOAP often being a little slower in operation than REST for a similar task. SOAP does, however, make a more complete job of separating the remote procedure call from its method of transport, as well as add a number of extra features and facilities, such as the Fault element and type checking via namespaces.

Summary

In this lesson we considered SOAP, the Simple Object Access Protocol. SOAP is a popular web service protocol with a rather different approach to the REST protocol utilized in Lesson 15.

Either style of web service can be used via XMLHTTPRequest requests, though they differ somewhat in the complexity of the code involved.

LESSON 17

A JavaScript Library for Ajax

In this lesson you will learn how to encapsulate some of the techniques studied up to now into a small JavaScript library that you can call from your applications.

An Ajax Library

Through the lessons and code examples up to now, we have developed a number of JavaScript code techniques for implementing the various parts of an Ajax application. Among these methods are:

- A method for generating an instance of the XMLHTTPRequest object, which works across the range of currently popular browsers

- Routines for building and sending GET and POST requests via the XMLHTTPRequest object

- Techniques for avoiding unwanted caching of GET requests

- A style of callback function that checks for correct completion of the XMLHTTPRequest call prior to carrying out your wishes

- Methods of providing user feedback

- Techniques for dealing with text data returned in responseText

- Techniques for dealing with XML information returned in responseXML

In addition, you saw in Lesson 13, "AHAH—Asynchronous HTML and HTTP," how some of these methods could be abstracted into a small JavaScript "library" (in that case containing only two functions).

This lesson extends that idea to build a more fully featured library that allows Ajax facilities to be added simply to an HTML page with minimal additional code.

Of necessity, our Ajax library will not be as complex or comprehensive as the open source projects described later in the book; however, it will be complete enough to use in the construction of functional Ajax applications.

Reviewing myAHAHlib.js

Listing 17.1 shows the code of myAHAHlib.js, reproduced from Lesson 13.

LISTING 17.1 myAHAHlib.js

```
function callAHAH(url, pageElement, callMessage) {
    document.getElementById(pageElement).innerHTML
 ➥ = callMessage;
    try {
    req = new XMLHttpRequest(); /* e.g. Firefox */
    } catch(e) {
      try {
      req = new ActiveXObject("Msxml2.XMLHTTP");
      /* some versions IE */
      } catch (e) {
        try {
        req = new ActiveXObject("Microsoft.XMLHTTP");
        /* some versions IE */
        } catch (E) {
         req = false;
        }
      }
    }
    req.onreadystatechange =
➥function() {responseAHAH(pageElement);};
    req.open("GET",url,true);
    req.send(null);
  }
```

```
function responseAHAH(pageElement) {
   var output = '';
   if(req.readyState == 4) {
      if(req.status == 200) {
         output = req.responseText;
         document.getElementById(pageElement).innerHTML
➥ = output;
      }
   }
}
```

Let's consider how we may extend the capabilities of this library:

- There is currently support only for HTTP GET requests. It would
  be useful to be able to support at least the HTTP POST request
  too, especially if you intend to build applications using the
  REST protocol (as described in Lesson 15, "Web Services and
  the REST Protocol").

- The library currently only deals with text information returned
  via responseText and has no means to deal with responseXML.

Implementing Our Library

Having identified what needs to be done, we'll now put together a more
capable Ajax library.

Creating XMLHTTPRequest Instances

Let's turn our attention first to the routine for creating instances of the
XMLHTTPRequest object.

Currently this function is coupled tightly with the routine for constructing
and sending HTTP GET requests. Let's decouple the part responsible for
the creation of the XMLHTTPRequest instance and put it into a function of
its own:

```
function createREQ() {
try {
     req = new XMLHttpRequest(); /* e.g. Firefox */
     } catch(err1) {
```

```
    try {
    req = new ActiveXObject("Msxml2.XMLHTTP");
    /* some versions IE */
    } catch (err2) {
      try {
      req = new ActiveXObject("Microsoft.XMLHTTP");
      /* some versions IE */
      } catch (err3) {
       req = false;
      }
    }
  }
  return req;
}
```

We can now create XMLHTTPRequest object instances by simply calling the following function:

```
var myreq = createREQ();
```

HTTP GET and POST Requests

We'll start with the GET request because we already support that type of request:

```
function requestGET(url, query, req) {
myRand=parseInt(Math.random()*99999999);
req.open("GET",url+'?'+query+'&rand='+myRand,true);
req.send(null);
}
```

To this request we must pass as arguments the URL to which the request will be sent and the identity of the XMLHTTPRequest object instance.

We could exclude the query argument because, in a GET request, it's encoded into the URL. We keep the two arguments separate here to maintain a similar interface to the function for making POST requests.

The query argument must be suitably encoded prior to calling the function, though the cache-busting random element is added by the function.

Next, the POST function:

```
function requestPOST(url, query, req) {
req.open("POST", url,true);
req.setRequestHeader('Content-Type',
➥'application/x-www-form-urlencoded');
req.send(query);
}
```

The Callback Function

How do we deal with the callback function? We are going to add a further function:

```
function doCallback(callback,item) {
eval(callback + '(item)');
}
```

This function uses JavaScript's eval() function to execute another function whose name is passed to it as an argument, while also passing to that function an argument of its own, via item.

Let's look at how these functions might interact when called from an event handler:

```
function doAjax(url,query,callback,reqtype,getxml) {
// create the XMLHTTPRequest object instance
var myreq = createREQ();
myreq.onreadystatechange = function() {
if(myreq.readyState == 4) {
   if(myreq.status == 200) {
     var item = myreq.responseText;
     if(getxml==1) {
        item = myreq.responseXML;
      }
   doCallback(callback, item);
   }
  }
}
if(reqtype=='post') {
requestPOST(url,query,myreq);
} else {
requestGET(url,query,myreq);
}
}
```

Our function doAjax now takes five arguments:

- url—The target URL for the Ajax call

- query—The encoded query string

- callback—Identity of the callback function

- reqtype—'post' or 'get'

- getxml—1 to get XML data, 0 for text

Listing 17.2 shows the complete JavaScript source code.

LISTING 17.2   The Ajax Library myAJAXlib.js

```
function createREQ() {
try {
    req = new XMLHttpRequest(); /* e.g. Firefox */
    } catch(err1) {
      try {
      req = new ActiveXObject("Msxml2.XMLHTTP");
  /* some versions IE */
      } catch (err2) {
        try {
        req = new ActiveXObject("Microsoft.XMLHTTP");
  /* some versions IE */
        } catch (err3) {
         req = false;
         }
       }
     }
     return req;
}

function requestGET(url, query, req) {
myRand=parseInt(Math.random()*99999999);
req.open("GET",url+'?'+query+'&rand='+myRand,true);
req.send(null);
}

function requestPOST(url, query, req) {
req.open("POST", url,true);
req.setRequestHeader('Content-Type', 'application/
x-www-form-urlencoded');
req.send(query);
}
```

```
function doCallback(callback,item) {
eval(callback + '(item)');
}

function doAjax(url,query,callback,reqtype,getxml) {
// create the XMLHTTPRequest object instance
var myreq = createREQ();

myreq.onreadystatechange = function() {
if(myreq.readyState == 4) {
   if(myreq.status == 200) {
       var item = myreq.responseText;
       if(getxml==1) {
           item = myreq.responseXML;
       }
       doCallback(callback, item);
   }
  }
}
if(reqtype=='post') {
requestPOST(url,query,myreq);
} else {
requestGET(url,query,myreq);
}
}
```

Using the Library

To demonstrate the use of the library, we're going to start with another simple HTML page, the code for which is shown here:

```
<html>
<head>
</head>
<body>
<form name="form1">
<input type="button" value="test">
</form>
</body>
</html>
```

This simple page displays only a button labeled "Test". All the functionality on the form will be created in JavaScript, using our new Ajax library.

The steps required to "Ajaxify" the application are

1. Include the Ajax library myAJAXlib.js in the <head> area of the page.

2. Write a callback function to deal with the returned information.

3. Add an event handler to the page to invoke the server call.

We'll start by demonstrating a GET request and using the information returned in the responseText property. This is similar to the situation we faced when dealing with AHAH in Lesson 13.

Including the Ajax library is straightforward:

```
<head>
<script Language="JavaScript" src="myAJAXlib.js"></script>
```

Next, we need to define our callback function to deal with the value stored in the responseText property. For these examples, we'll simply display the returned text in an alert:

```
<head>
<script Language="JavaScript" src="myAJAXlib.js"></script>
<script Language="JavaScript">
function cback(text) {
alert(text);
}
</script>
```

Finally, we need to add an event handler call to our button:

```
onClick="doAjax('libtest.php','param=hello',
➥'cback','get','0')"
```

Our server-side script libtest.php simply echoes back the parameter sent as the second argument:

```
<?php
echo "Parameter value was ".$param;
?>
```

Meanwhile the remaining parameters of the function call declare that the callback function is called cback, that we want to send an HTTP GET request, and that we expect the returned data to be in responseText.

Listing 17.3 shows the complete code of our revised HTML page.

LISTING 17.3   HTML Page Rewritten to Call myAJAXlib.js

```
<html>
<head>
<script Language="JavaScript" src="myAJAXlib.js">
➥</script>
<script Language="JavaScript">
function cback(text) {
alert(text);
}
</script>
</head>
<body>
<form name="form1">
<input type="button" value="test" onClick=
➥"doAjax('libtest.php','param-hello',
➥'cback','get','0')">
</form>
</body>
</html>
```

Figure 17.1 shows the result of running the program.

FIGURE 17.1   Returning text following an HTTP GET request.

To use the same library to retrieve XML data, we'll once again use the server-side script of Lesson 11, "Our First Ajax Application," which you may recall delivers the current server time in a small XML document:

```
<?php
header('Content-Type: text/xml');
echo "<?xml version=\"1.0\" ?><clock1><timenow>"
➥.date('H:i:s')."</timenow></clock1>";
?>
```

Our callback function must be modified because we now need to return the parsed XML. We'll use some DOM methods that should by now be familiar:

```
<script>
function cback(text) {
var servertime = text.getElementsByTagName("timenow")[0]
➥.childNodes[0].nodeValue;
alert('Server time is '+servertime);
}
</script>
```

The only other thing we need to change is the call to our doAjax() function:

```
onClick="doAjax('telltimeXML.php','','cback','post','1')"
```

Here we have decided to make a POST request. Our server-side script telltimeXML.php does not require a query string, so in this case the second argument is left blank. The final parameter has been set to '1' indicating that we expect the server to respond with XML in the property responseXML.

Figure 17.2 shows the result of running the program.

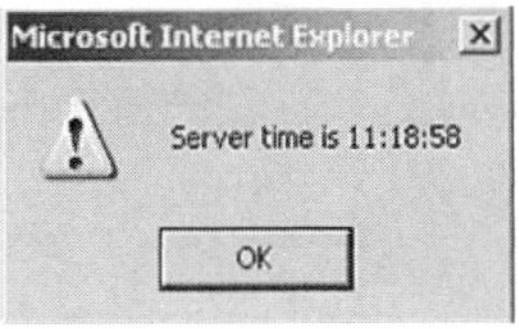

FIGURE 17.2   Returning the server time in XML via a POST request.

Extending the Library

The current library might be improved in a number of ways. These will be left as an exercise for the reader, though in many cases the techniques have been covered elsewhere in the book.

User feedback, for example, has not been addressed; we previously discussed how the display of suitable text or a graphic image can alert the user that a request is currently in progress. It would be useful to revise the library to include the techniques discussed in Lesson 11 and elsewhere.

Error handling, too, has been excluded from the code and would prove a useful addition. For example, it should not be too difficult to modify the library to detect XMLHTTPRequest status properties other than 200 and output a suitable error message to the user.

Feel free to experiment with the code and see what you can achieve.

Summary

This lesson combined many of the techniques discussed to date to produce a compact and reusable JavaScript library that can be called simply from an HTML page.

The code supports both HTTP GET and HTTP POST requests and can deal with data returned from the server as text or XML.

Using such a library allows Ajax to be introduced to web pages using relatively small additions to the HTML markup. This not only keeps the code clean and easy to read but also simplifies the addition of Ajax facilities to upgrade legacy HTML.

In Lesson 18, "Ajax 'Gotchas,'" the last lesson of Part III, we'll discuss some potential problems and pitfalls awaiting the programmer in developing Ajax applications.

LESSON 18

Ajax "Gotchas"

In this lesson you'll learn about some of the common Ajax mistakes and how to avoid them.

Common Ajax Errors

Ajax has some common pitfalls waiting to catch the unwary developer. In this lesson, the last lesson of Part III, we'll review some of these pitfalls and discuss possible approaches to finding solutions.

The list is not exhaustive, and the solutions offered are not necessarily appropriate for every occasion. They should, however, provide some food for thought.

The Back Button

All browsers in common use have a Back button on the navigation bar. The browser maintains a list of recently visited pages in memory and allows you to step back through these to revisit pages you have recently seen.

Users have become used to the Back button as a standard part of the surfing experience, just as they have with the other facets of the page-based web paradigm.

Ajax, as you have learned, does much to shake off the idea of web-based information being delivered in separate, page-sized chunks; with an Ajax application, you may be able to change page content over and over again without any thought of reloading the browser display with a whole new page.

> **Tip** JavaScript has its own equivalent of the Back
> button written into the language. The statements
>
> ```
> onClick = "history.back()"
> ```
>
> and
>
> ```
> onClick = "history.go(-1)"
> ```
>
> both mimic the action of clicking the Back button
> once.

What then of the Back button?

This issue has caused considerable debate among developers recently.
There seem to be two main schools of thought:

- Create a means of recording state programmatically, and use that
  to re-create a previous state when the Back button is pressed.

- Persuade users that the Back button is no longer necessary.

Artificially re-creating former states is indeed possible but adds a great
deal of complexity to Ajax code and is therefore somewhat the province
of the braver programmer!

Although the latter option sounds a bit like it's trying to avoid the issue, it
does perhaps have some merit. If you use Ajax to re-create desktop-like
user interfaces, it's worthy of note that desktop applications generally
don't have—or need—a Back button because the notion of separate
"pages" never enters the user's head!

Bookmarking and Links

This problem is not unrelated to the Back button issue.

When you bookmark a page, you are attempting to save a shortcut to
some content. In the page-based metaphor, this is not unreasonable;
although pages can have some degree of dynamic content, being able

subsequently to find the page itself usually gets us close enough to seeing what we saw on our previous visit.

Ajax, however, can use the same page address for a whole application, with large quantities of dynamic content being returned from the server in accordance with a user's actions.

What happens when you want to bookmark a particular screen of information and/or pass that link to a friend or colleague? Merely using the URL of the current page is unlikely to produce the results you require.

Although it may be difficult to totally eradicate this problem, it may be possible to alleviate it somewhat by providing permanent links to specially chosen states of an application.

Telling the User That Something Is Happening

This is another issue somewhat related to the change of interface style away from separate pages.

The user who is already familiar with browsing web pages may have become accustomed to program activity coinciding with the loading of a new or revised page.

Many Ajax applications therefore provide some consistent visual clue that activity is happening; perhaps a stationary graphic image might be replaced by an animated version, the cursor style might change, or a pop-up message appear. Some of these techniques have been mentioned in some of the lessons in this book.

Making Ajax Degrade Elegantly

The lessons in this book have covered the development of Ajax applications using various modern browsers. It is still possible, though, that a user might surprise you by attempting to use your application with a browser that is too old to support the necessary technologies. Alternatively, a visitor's browser may have JavaScript and/or ActiveX disabled (for security or other reasons).

It is unfortunate if an Ajax application should break down under these conditions.

At the least, the occurrence of obvious errors (such as a failure to create an instance of the XMLHTTPRequest object) should be reported to the user. If the Ajax application is so complex that it cannot be made to automatically revert to a non-Ajax mode of operation, perhaps the user can at least be redirected to a non-Ajax version of the application.

> **Tip** You can detect whether JavaScript is unavailable by using the <noscript> ... </noscript> tags in your HTML page. Statements between these tags are evaluated only if JavaScript is NOT available:
>
> ```
> <noscript>
> JavaScript is not available in this browser.<br />
> Please go <a href="otherplace.htm">HERE</a> for
> the HTML-only version.<br />
> </noscript>
> ```

Dealing with Search Engine Spiders

Search engines gather information about websites through various means, an important one being the use of automated programs called *spiders*.

Spiders, as their name suggests, "crawl the web" by reading web pages and following links, building a database of content and other relevant information about particular websites. This database, better known as an *index*, is queried by search engine visitors using their key words and phrases and returns suggestions of relevant pages for them to visit.

This can create a problem for highly dynamic sites, which rely on user interaction (rather than passive surfing) to invoke the loading of new content delivered on-demand by the server. The visiting spider may not have access to the content that would be loaded by dynamic means and therefore never gets to index it.

The problem can be exacerbated further by the use of Ajax, with its tendency to deliver even more content in still fewer pages.

It would seem wise to ensure that spiders can index a static version of all relevant content somewhere on the site. Because spiders follow links embedded in pages, the provision of a hypertext linked site map can be a useful addition in this regard.

Pointing Out Active Page Elements

Without careful design, it may not be apparent to users which items on the page they can click on or otherwise interface with to make something happen.

It is worth trying to use a consistent style throughout an application to show which page elements cause server requests or some other dynamic activity. This is somewhat reminiscent of the way that hypertext links in HTML pages tend to be styled differently than plain text so that it's clear to a user that they perform an additional function.

At the expense of a little more coding effort, instructions and information about active elements can be incorporated in ToolTip-style pop-ups. This is, of course, especially important when a click on an active link can have a major effect on the application's state. Figure 18.1 shows an example of such a pop-up information box.

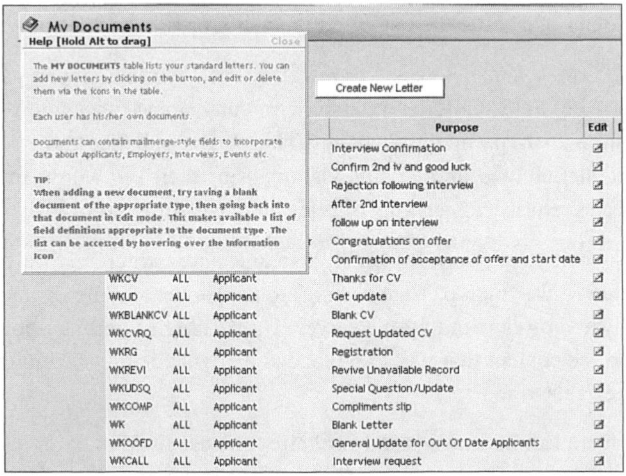

FIGURE 18.1   Pop-up information helps users to understand interfaces.

Don't Use Ajax Where It's Inappropriate

Attractive as Ajax undoubtedly is for improving web interfaces, you need to accept that there are many situations where the use of Ajax detracts from the user experience instead of adding to it.

This is especially true where the page-based interface metaphor is perfectly adequate for, perhaps even of greater relevance to, the content and style of the site. Text-based sites with subjects split conveniently into chapter-styled pages can often benefit as much from intelligently designed hyperlinking as they can from the addition of Ajax functionality.

Small sites in particular may struggle to get sufficient benefit from an Ajax interface to balance the associated costs of additional code and added complexity.

Security

Ajax does not itself seem to present any security issues that are not already present when designing web applications. It is notable, however, that Ajax-enhanced applications tend to contain more client-side code than they did previously.

Because the content of client-side code can be viewed easily by any user of the application, it is important that sensitive information not be revealed within it. In this context, sensitive information is not limited to such things as usernames and passwords (though they are, of course, sensitive), but also includes business logic. Make the server-side scripts responsible for carrying out such issues as database connection. Validate data on the server before applying it to any important processing.

Test Code Across Multiple Platforms

It will be clear from the content of this book that the various browsers behave differently in their implementation of JavaScript. The major difference in the generation of XMLHTTPRequest object instances between Microsoft and non-Microsoft browsers is a fundamental example, but there is a host of minor differences, too.

The DOM, in particular, is handled rather differently, not only between browsers but also between different versions of the same browser. CSS implementation is another area where minor differences still proliferate.

Although it has always been important to test new applications on various browsers, this is perhaps more important than ever when faced with the added complexity of Ajax applications.

Hopefully browsers will continue to become more standards-compliant, but until then test applications on as many different platforms and with as many different browsers as possible.

Ajax Won't Cure a Bad Design

All the dynamic interactivity in the world won't correct a web application with a design that is fundamentally flawed.

All the tenets of good web design still apply to Ajax applications:

- Write for multiple browsers and validate your code.

- Comment and document your code well so that you can debug it later.

- Use small graphics wherever possible so that they load quickly.

- Make sure that your choices of colors, backgrounds, font sizes, and styles don't make pages difficult to read.

> **Tip**   The W3C offers a free online validator at
> http://validator.w3.org/.

Some Programming Gotchas

Some of these have been alluded to in various lessons, but it's worth grouping them here. These are probably the most common programming issues that Ajax developers bump up against at some time or other!

Browser Caching of GET Requests

Making repeated GET requests to the same URL can often lead to the response coming not from the server but from the browser cache. This problem seems especially significant when using Internet Explorer.

Although in theory this can be cured with the use of suitable HTTP headers, in practice the cache can be stubborn.

An effective way of sidestepping this problem is to add a random element to the URL to which the request is sent; the browser interprets this as a request to a different page and returns a server page rather than a cached version.

In the text we achieved this by adding a random number. Another approach favored by many is to add a number derived from the time, which will of course be different every time:

```
var url = "serverscript.php"+"?rand="+new Date().getTime();
```

Permission Denied Errors

Receiving a Permission Denied error usually means that you have fallen foul of the security measure preventing cross-domain requests from being made by an XMLHTTPRequest object.

Calls must be made to server programs existing in the same domain as the calling script.

 Caution   Be careful that the domain is written in exactly the same way. Somedomain.com may be interpreted as referring to a different domain from www.somedomain.com, and permission will be denied.

Escaping Content

When constructing queries for GET or POST requests, remember to escape variables that could contain spaces or other nontext characters. In the following code, the value `idValue` has been collected from a text input field on a form, so we escape it to ensure correct encoding:

```
http.open("GET", url + escape(idValue) + "&rand=" + myRandom,
true);
```

Summary

Ajax undoubtedly has the potential to greatly improve web interfaces. However, the paradigm change from traditional page-based interfaces to highly dynamic applications has created a few potholes for developers to step into. In this lesson we've tried to round up a few of the better-known ones.

Some of these issues have already been encountered in the other lessons in this book, whereas others will perhaps not become apparent until you start to develop real-world applications.

This lesson concludes Part III, "More Complex Ajax Technologies." If you have followed the lessons through to this point, you will by now have a good grip on the fundamentals of the `XMLHTTPRequest` object, JavaScript, XML, and the Document Object Model, and be capable of creating useful Ajax applications from first principles.

Fortunately, you don't have to always work from first principles. Many open source and commercial projects on the Internet offer a wide variety of Ajax frameworks, tools, and resources.

Part IV, "Commercial and Open Source Ajax Resources," of the book concludes our journey through Ajax development by looking at some of these resources and their capabilities.

LESSON 19

The prototype.js Toolkit

In this lesson you will learn about the prototype.js JavaScript library and how it can reduce the work required for building capable Ajax applications.

Introducing prototype.js

Part IV, "Commercial and Open Source Ajax Resources," looks at some available code libraries and frameworks for Ajax development.

We begin this lesson with Sam Stephenson's *prototype.js*, a popular JavaScript library containing an array of functions useful in the development of cross-browser JavaScript routines, and including specific support for Ajax. You'll see how your JavaScript code can be simplified by using this library's powerful support for DOM manipulation, HTML forms, and the XMLHTTPRequest object.

The latest version of the prototype.js library can be downloaded from http://prototype.conio.net/.

 Caution At the time of writing, prototype.js is at version 1.4.0. If you download a different version, check the documentation to see whether there are differences between your version and the one described here.

Including the library in your web application is simple, just include in the <head> section of your HTML document the line:

```
<script src="prototype.js" Language="JavaScript"
➥type="text/javascript"></script>
```

prototype.js contains a broad range of functions that can make writing JavaScript code quicker, and the resulting scripts cleaner and easier to maintain.

The library includes general-purpose functions providing shortcuts to regular programming tasks, a wrapper for HTML forms, an object to encapsulate the XMLHTTPRequest object, methods and objects for simplifying DOM tasks, and more.

Let's take a look at some of these tools.

The $() Function

$() is essentially a shortcut to the getElementById() DOM method. Normally, to return the value of a particular element you would use an expression such as

```
var mydata = document.getElementById('someElementID');
```

The $() function simplifies this task by returning the value of the element whose ID is passed to it as an argument:

```
var mydata = $('someElementID');
```

Furthermore, $() (unlike getElementById()) can accept multiple element IDs as an argument and return an array of the associated element values. Consider this line of code:

```
mydataArray = $('id1','id2','id3');
```

In this example:

- mydataArray[0] contains value of element with ID id1.

- mydataArray[1] contains value of element with ID id2.

- mydataArray[2] contains value of element with ID id3.

The $F() Function

The $F() function returns the value of a form input field when the input element or its ID is passed to it as an argument. Look at the following HTML snippet:

```
<input type="text" id="input1" name="input1">
<select id="input2" name="input2">
 <option value="0">Option A</option>
 <option value="1">Option B</option>
 <option value="2">Option C</option>
</select>
```

Here we could use

```
$F('input1')
```

to return the value in the text box and

```
$F('input2')
```

to return the value of the currently selected option of the select box. The $F() function works equally well on check box and text area input elements, making it easy to return the element values regardless of the input element type.

The Form Object

prototype.js defines a Form object having several useful methods for simplifying HTML form manipulation.

You can return an array of a form's input fields by calling the getElements() method:

```
inputs = Form.getElements('thisform');
```

The serialize() method allows input names and values to be formatted into a URL-compatible list:

```
inputlist = Form.serialize('thisform');
```

Using the preceding line of code, the variable inputlist would now contain a string of serialized parameter and value pairs:

```
field1=value1&field2=value2&field3=value3…
```

`Form.disable('thisform')` and `Form.enable('thisform')` each do exactly what it says on the tin.

The `Try.these()` Function

Previous lessons discussed the use of exceptions to enable you to catch runtime errors and deal with them cleanly. The `Try.these()` function provides a convenient way to encapsulate these methods to provide a cross-browser solution where JavaScript implementation details differ:

```
return Try.these(function1(),function2(),function3(), …);
```

The functions are processed in sequence, operation moving on to the next function when an error condition causes an exception to be thrown. Operation stops when any of the functions completes successfully, at which point the function returns `true`.

Applying this function to the creation of an `XMLHTTPRequest` instance shows the simplicity of the resulting code:

```
return Try.these(
    function() {return new ActiveXObject('Msxml2.XMLHTTP')},
    function() {return new ActiveXObject('Microsoft.XMLHTTP')},
    function() {return new XMLHttpRequest()}
    )
```

 Note You may want to compare this code snippet with Listing 8.1 to see just how much code complexity has been reduced and readability improved.

Wrapping `XMLHTTPRequest`—the `Ajax` Object

prototype.js defines an `Ajax` object designed to simplify the development of your JavaScript code when building Ajax applications. This object has a number of classes that encapsulate the code you need to send server requests, monitor their progress, and deal with the returned data.

Ajax.Request

`Ajax.Request` deals with the details of creating an instance of the `XMLHTTPRequest` object and sending a correctly formatted request. Calling it is straightforward:

```
var myAjax = new Ajax.Request( url, {method: 'post',
➥parameters: mydata, onComplete: responsefunction} );
```

In this call, `url` defines the location of the server resource to be called, `method` may be either `post` or `get`, `mydata` is a serialized string containing the request parameters, and `responsefunction` is the name of the callback function that handles the server response.

> **Tip**   The second argument is constructed using a notation often called *JSON (JavaScript Object Notation)*. The argument is built up from a series of `parameter:value` pairs, the whole contained within braces. The parameter values themselves may be JSON objects, arrays, or simple values.
>
> JSON is popular as a data interchange protocol due to its ease of construction, ease of parsing, and language independence. You can find out more about it at http://www.json.org.

The `onComplete` parameter is one of several options corresponding to the possible values of the `XMLHTTPRequest` `readyState` properties, in this case a `readyState` value of 4 (`Complete`). You might instead specify that the callback function should execute during the prior phases `Loading`, `Loaded`, or `Interactive`, by using the associated parameters `onLoading`, `onLoaded`, or `onInteractive`.

There are several other optional parameters, including

```
asynchronous:false
```

to indicate that a server call should be made synchronously. The default value for the `asynchronous` option is `true`.

Ajax.Updater

On occasions when you require the returned data to update a page element, the Ajax.Updater class can simplify the task. All you need to do is to specify which element should be updated:

```
var myAjax = new Ajax.Updater(elementID, url, options);
```

The call is somewhat similar to that for Ajax.Request but with the addition of the target element's ID as the first argument. The following is a code example of Ajax.Updater:

```
<script>
  function updateDIV(mydiv)
  {
      var url = 'http://example.com/serverscript.php';
      var params = 'param1=value1&param2=value2';
      var myAjax = new Ajax.Updater
              (
              mydiv,
              url,
              {method: 'get', parameters: params}
              );

  }
</script>
<input type="button" value="Go"
onclick="updateDIV(targetDiv)">
<div id="targetDiv"></div>
```

Once again, several additional options may be used when making the call. A noteworthy one is the addition of

```
evalscripts:true
```

to the options list. With this option added, any JavaScript code returned by the server will be evaluated.

Ajax.PeriodicalUpdater

The Ajax.PeriodicalUpdater class can be used to repeatedly create an Ajax.Updater instance. In this way you can have a page element updated after a certain time interval has elapsed. This can be useful for such applications as a stock market ticker or an RSS reader because it ensures that the visitor is always viewing reasonably up-to-date information.

`Ajax.PeriodicalUpdater` adds two further parameters to the `Ajax.Updater` options:

- frequency—The delay in seconds between successive updates. Default is two seconds.

- decay—The multiplier by which successive delays are increased if the server should return unchanged data. Default value is 1, which leaves the delay constant.

Here's an example call to `Ajax.PeriodicalUpdater`:

```
var myAjax = new Ajax.PeriodicalUpdater(elementID, url,
➥{frequency: 3.0, decay: 2.0});
```

Here we elected to set the initial delay to 3 seconds and have this delay double in length each time unchanged data is returned by the server.

Example Project—Stock Price Reader

Let's use the prototype.js library to build a simple reader that updates periodically to show the latest value returned from the server. In this example, we'll use a simple server-side script `rand.php` to simulate a changing stock price:

```
<?php
srand ((double) microtime( )*1000000);
$price = 50 + rand(0,5000)/100;
echo "$price";
?>
```

This script first initializes PHP's random number routine by calling the `srand()` function and passing it an argument derived from the current time. The `rand(0,5000)` function is then used to generate a random number that is manipulated arithmetically to produce phony "stock prices" in the range 50.00 to 100.00.

Now let's build a simple HTML page to display the current stock price. This page forms the basis for our Ajax application:

```
<!DOCTYPE HTML PUBLIC "-//W3C//DTD HTML 4.01 Transitional//EN"
➥"http://www.w3.org/TR/html4/loose.dtd">
<html>
<head>
<script src="prototype.js" Language="JavaScript"
➥type="text/javascript"></script>
<title>Stock Reader powered by Prototype.js</title>
</head>
<body>
<h2>Stock Reader</h2>
<h4>Powered by Prototype.js</h4>
<p>Current Stock Price:</p>
<div id="price"></div>
</body>
</html>
```

Note that we included the prototype.js library by means of a <script> tag in the document head. We also defined a <div> with id set to "price", which will be used to display the current stock price.

We now need to implement the Ajax.PeriodicalUpdater class, which we'll attach to the document body element's onLoad event handler. Listing 19.1 shows the complete script.

LISTING 19.1   Ajax Stock Price Reader Using prototype.js

```
<!DOCTYPE HTML PUBLIC "-//W3C//DTD HTML 4.01
➥ Transitional//EN"
➥"http://www.w3.org/TR/html4/loose.dtd">
<html>
<head>
<script src="prototype.js" Language="JavaScript"
➥type="text/javascript"></script>
<script>
function checkprice()
{
var myAjax = new Ajax.PeriodicalUpdater('price',
➥'rand.php', {method: 'post', frequency: 3.0,
➥ decay: 1});
}
</script>
<title>Stock Reader powered by Prototype.js</title>
```

```
</head>
<body onLoad="checkprice()">
<h2>Stock Reader</h2>
<h4>Powered by Prototype.js</h4>
<p>Current Stock Price:</p>
<div id="price"></div>
</body>
</html>
```

Look how simple the code for the application has become through using prototype.js. Implementing the application is merely a matter of defining a one-line function checkprice() to instantiate our repeating Ajax call and calling that function from the body element's onLoad event handler.

From the arguments passed to Ajax.PeriodicalUpdater, you'll see that a 3-second repeat interval has been specified. This period does not change with subsequent calls because the decay value has been set to 1.

Figure 19.1 shows the application running. What cannot be seen from the figure, of course, is the stock price updating itself every 3 seconds to show a new value.

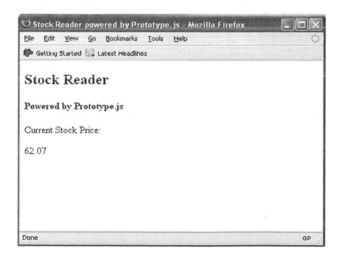

FIGURE 19.1 Ajax stock reader.

This simple example does not come close to showing off the power and versatility of the prototype.js library. Rather, it is intended to get you started with your own experiments by offering an easy point of access to this great resource.

Summary

In this first lesson in Part IV of the book, we discussed the use of the powerful and elegant prototype.js JavaScript library.

The functions made available by this library greatly simplify some of the trickier programming tasks when developing Ajax applications.

The library offers good support for the `XMLHTTPRequest` object, along with time-saving shortcuts for DOM handling, HTML forms, and many other techniques relevant to Ajax development.

LESSON 20
Using Rico

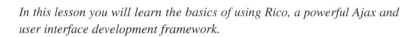

In this lesson you will learn the basics of using Rico, a powerful Ajax and user interface development framework.

Introducing Rico

In Lesson 19, "The prototype.js Toolkit," we looked at prototype.js, a powerful and useful JavaScript library that simplifies many of the programming tasks facing the Ajax developer.

In this lesson we'll take a look at using Rico, a sophisticated Ajax framework employing the prototype.js library.

Rico is an open source library that extends the capabilities of prototype.js to provide a rich set of interface development tools. In addition to the Ajax development techniques discussed so far, Rico offers a whole range of tools such as drag-and-drop, cinematic effects, and more.

> **Tip** *Rico* is the Spanish word for *rich*, which seems appropriate for a toolkit designed for building rich user interfaces!

Using Rico in Your Applications

To start using Rico to build applications with rich user interfaces, you need to include both Rico and prototype.js libraries in the `<head>`…`</head>` section of your web pages.

```
<script src="scripts/prototype.js"></script>
<script src="scripts/rico.js"></script>
```

Rico's `AjaxEngine`

The inclusion of rico.js causes an instance called `ajaxEngine` of an `AjaxEngine` object to be created automatically ready for you to use. The `AjaxEngine` is Rico's mechanism for adding Ajax capabilities to your web pages.

The `AjaxEngine` requires a three-step process to update page elements via Ajax:

1. Register the request handler. Registering the request handler associates a unique name with a particular URL to be called via Ajax.

2. Register the response handler. Rico can deal with the return of both HTML data and JavaScript code within the XML returned from the server. In the former case, the response handler identifies a page element that is to be updated using the returned data; in the latter case, a JavaScript object that handles the server response.

3. Make the Ajax call from the page by using an appropriate event handler.

We first register our request handler by making a call to the `registerRequest()` method of `ajaxEngine`:

```
ajaxEngine.registerRequest('getData','getData.php');
```

We have now associated the name `getData` with a request to the server routine `getData.php`. That server-side routine is required to return a response in well-formed XML. The following is an example of a typical response:

```
<ajax-response>
   <response type="element" id="showdata">
     <div class="datadisplay">
        The <b>cat</b> sat on the <b>mat</b>
     </div>
   </response>
</ajax-response>
```

Such responses always have a root element `<ajax-response>`. The `<response>` element it contains in this example has two attributes, type `element` and id `showdata`. These signify, respectively, that the response contains HTML, and that this HTML is to be used to update the page element having id `showdata`. This element is updated via its `innerHTML` property.

> **Tip**   Rico is capable of updating multiple page elements from one request. To achieve this, the `<ajax-response>` element may contain multiple `<response>` elements.

The other form of response that Rico can return is a JavaScript object. Here's an example:

```
<ajax-response>
  <response type="object" id="myHandler">
    <sentence>The cat sat on the mat.</sentence>
  </response>
</ajax-response>
```

Here the type has been set to `object`, indicating that the content is to be dealt with by a JavaScript object, the identity of which is contained in the id value (here `myHandler`). The content of the response is always passed to the `ajaxUpdate` method of this object.

How the response handler is registered depends on which type of response we are dealing with. For responses of type `element`, you can simply call:

```
ajaxEngine.registerAjaxElement('showdata');
```

In the case of responses containing a JavaScript object, you will need:

```
ajaxEngine.registerAjaxObject('myHandler', new myHandler());
```

Whereas responses of type `element` are simply intended for the updating of HTML page elements, responses of type `object` can have handlers to process responses in any way they want. This allows Rico applications to be built ranging from simple to sophisticated.

A Simple Example

We can see Rico in action by using the simple script of Listing 20.1. This application updates two HTML elements with a single call to Rico's ajaxEngine object. The script for the application is in Listing 20.1.

LISTING 20.1 A Simple Rico Application

```
<!DOCTYPE HTML PUBLIC "-//W3C//DTD HTML 4.01
➥ Transitional//EN"
➥"http://www.w3.org/TR/html4/loose.dtd">
<html>
<head>
<title>Testing OpenRico</title>
<script src="prototype.js"></script>
<script src="rico.js"></script>
<script type="text/javascript">
function callRICO()
{
ajaxEngine.registerRequest('myRequest', 'ricotest.php');
ajaxEngine.registerAjaxElement('display');
ajaxEngine.registerAjaxElement('heading');
}
</script>
</head>
<body onload=" callRICO();">
<div id="heading"><h3>Demonstrating Rico</h3></div>
<input type="button" value="Get Server Data"
➥ onclick="ajaxEngine.sendRequest('myRequest');"/>
<div id="display"><p>This text should be replaced with
➥server data ...</p></div>
</body>
</html>
```

You will see from the code that the single function callRICO() is used to register both the single request handler myRequest and two response handlers. The response handlers are used to update two <div> containers; one of these contains the page's heading, the other a short text message. On making the Rico request, the contents of both are updated, leaving the page with a new title and now displaying some server information instead of the previous text message. Figure 20.1 shows before and after screenshots.

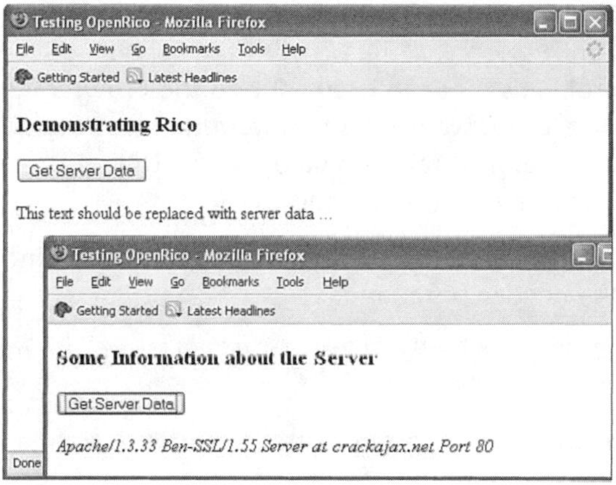

FIGURE 20.1 Updating multiple page elements with Rico.

The server routine is a simple PHP script that outputs the required XML data. The script uses PHP's $_SERVER['SERVER_SIGNATURE'] global variable. Note that the script constructs and returns two separate <response> elements, each responsible for updating a particular element in the HTML page.

Listing 20.2 shows the server script.

LISTING 20.2 The Server Script for Generating
<ajax-response>

```
<?php
header("Content-Type:text/xml");
header("Cache-Control:no-cache");
header("Pragma:no-cache");
echo "<ajax-response><response type=\"element\"
➥id=\"display\"><p>"
➥.$_SERVER['SERVER_SIGNATURE']
➥."</p></response>
➥<response type=\"element\" id=\"heading\">
➥<h3>Some Information about the Server</h3>
➥</response></ajax-response>";
?>
```

> **Tip**   Lesson 9, "Talking with the Server," discussed problems that can occur due to the browser cache. In that lesson we used a workaround involving adding a parameter of random value to the URL of the server resource that we wanted to call.
>
> This script example uses another technique, including the header commands
>
> ```
> header("Cache-Control:no-cache");
> header("Pragma:no-cache");
> ```
>
> instructing the browser not to cache this page, but to collect a new copy from the server each time.

> **Caution**   PHP's $_SERVER global array variable was introduced in PHP 4.1.0. If you have an older version of PHP installed, you'll need the global variable $HTTP_SERVER_VARS instead.

Rico's Other Interface Tools

Rico's capabilities aren't limited to aiding the development of Ajax applications. Let's now look at some other capabilities you can add to your user interfaces using the Rico toolkit. Although these techniques do not themselves use Ajax, it takes little imagination to realize what they might achieve when combined with Rico's Ajax tools.

Drag-and-Drop

Both desktop applications and the operating systems on which they run make widespread use of drag-and-drop to simplify the user interface. The JavaScript techniques required to implement drag-and-drop can be tricky to master, not least because of the many cross-browser issues that arise.

Drag-and-drop using Rico, however, is simple.

Including the rico.js file in your application automatically causes the creation of an object called dndMgr, Rico's Drag and Drop Manager. Using the dndMgr object is much like using AjaxEngine; this time, though, we need to register not Ajax requests and responses, but *draggable* items and *drop zones* (page elements that can receive dragged items).

These tasks are carried out via the registerDraggable and registerDropZone methods:

```
dndMgr.registerDraggable( new Rico.Draggable('test',
➥'dragElementID') );
dndMgr.registerDropZone( new Rico.Dropzone
➥('dropElementID') );
```

These two simple commands declare, respectively, a page element with ID dragElementID as being draggable, and another element with ID dropElementID as a drop zone. The argument 'test' of the registerDraggable() method defines a type for the draggable item, which can be tested and used by subsequent code, if required.

Example of a Drag-and-Drop Interface

Listing 20.3 shows how simple it is to implement drag-and-drop using Rico. The displayed HTML page is shown in Figure 20.2.

LISTING 20.3 Simple Drag-and-Drop Using Rico

```
<!DOCTYPE HTML PUBLIC "-//W3C//DTD HTML 4.01
➥ Transitional//EN"
➥"http://www.w3.org/TR/html4/loose.dtd">
 <html>
<head>
  <script src="prototype.js"></script>
  <script src="rico.js"></script>
  <style>
  body {
  font: 10px normal arial, helvetica, verdana;
  background-color:#dddddd;
  }

  div.simpleDropPanel {
   width    : 260px;
   height   : 180px;
```

continues

LISTING 20.3   Continued

```
  background-color: #ffffff;
  padding  : 5px;
  border   : 1px solid #333333;
  }

  div.box {
  width           : 200px;
  cursor          : hand;
  background-color: #ffffff;
  -moz-opacity     : 0.6;
  filter                : alpha(Opacity=60);
  border: 1px solid #333333;
  }
  </style>
</head>
<body>
<table width="550">
<tr>
  <td><h3>Drag and Drop</h3>
  <p>Drag and drop data items into the target fields
➥using the left mouse button in the usual way.
➥Note how available target fields change colour
➥during the drag operation.</p>
  <p>Reload the page to start again.</p>
  <div class="box" id="draggable1">This is a piece
➥of draggable data</div>
  <div class="box" id="draggable2">
➥This is another</div>
  <div class="box" id="draggable3">
➥And this is a third</div>
  <br/>
  <table>
  <tr>
    <td>
      <div id="droponme" class="simpleDropPanel">
          <b>Drop Zone 1</b><br />A simple text area
      </div>
    </td>
    <td>
      <b>Drop Zone 2</b><br />
      A form text entry field.
      <form><textarea name="dropzone" id="droponme2"
➥ rows="6" cols="30"></textarea></form>
    </td>
  </tr>
```

```
   </table>
   </td>
</tr>
</table>
<script>
   dndMgr.registerDraggable( new
➥Rico.Draggable('foo','draggable1') );
   dndMgr.registerDraggable( new
➥Rico.Draggable('foo','draggable2') );
   dndMgr.registerDraggable( new Rico.
➥Draggable('foo','draggable3') );
   dndMgr.registerDropZone( new Rico.Dropzone
➥('droponme') );
   dndMgr.registerDropZone( new Rico.Dropzone
➥('droponme2') );
</script>
</body>
</html>
```

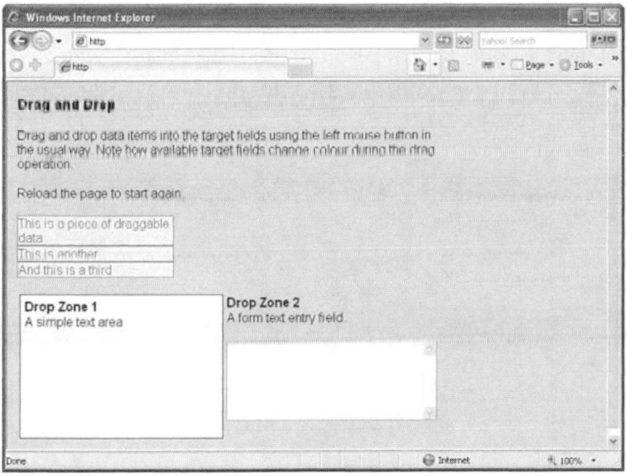

FIGURE 20.2   The simple drag-and-drop application.

The two JavaScript libraries rico.js and prototype.js are included in the
<head> of the document along with style definitions for various page ele-
ments.

Note that two page elements in particular, a <div> container and a <textarea> input field, have been given IDs of dropzone1 and dropzone2. Further down the listing, these two elements are defined as drop zones for our drag-and-drop operations by the lines

```
dndMgr.registerDropZone( new Rico.Dropzone('droponme') );
dndMgr.registerDropZone( new Rico.Dropzone('droponme2') );
```

You'll see too that three small <div> containers have been defined in the page and given IDs of draggable1, draggable2, and draggable3. As you have no doubt guessed, they are to become draggable page elements and are defined as such by the following code lines:

```
dndMgr.registerDraggable( new Rico.Draggable('foo',
➥'draggable1') );
dndMgr.registerDraggable( new Rico.Draggable('foo',
➥'draggable2') );
dndMgr.registerDraggable( new Rico.Draggable('foo',
➥'draggable3') );
```

That's all there is to it! Rico takes care of all the details, even changing the look of the available drop zones while something is being dragged, as shown in Figure 20.3.

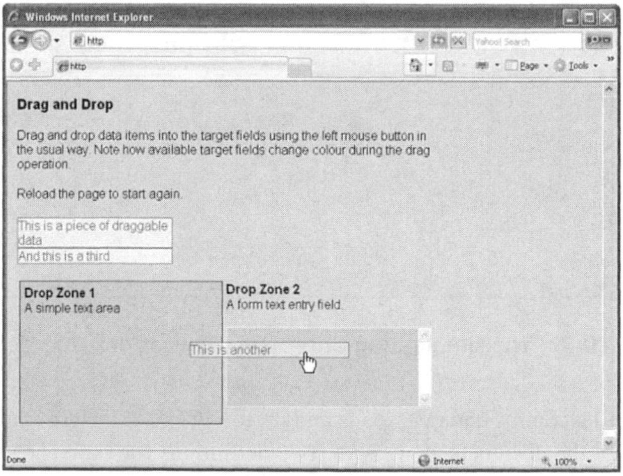

FIGURE 20.3 Drop zones highlighted during drag operation.

When released above an available drop zone, draggable items position themselves inline with the HTML code of the drop zone element, as can be seen in Figure 20.4.

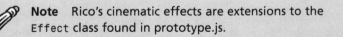

FIGURE 20.4 After completing the drag-and-drop.

Cinematic Effects

In addition to Ajax and drag-and-drop tools, Rico also makes available a host of user interface gadgets known collectively as *cinematic effects*.

> **Note** Rico's cinematic effects are extensions to the `Effect` class found in prototype.js.

These effects include animation of page elements (changing their sizes and/or shapes), fading effects (altering the opacity of page elements), applying rounded corners to objects, and manipulating object colors.

Used alongside the interface techniques previously discussed, these effects can help you to build sophisticated, eye-catching, and user-friendly interfaces much more reminiscent of desktop applications than of web pages.

Summary

Following our examination of the prototype.js library in the Lesson 19, this lesson moved on to experiment with Rico. Rico is an open source framework based on prototype.js that offers a simple way to integrate Ajax, along with drag-and-drop and other visual effects, into user interface designs.

Finally, in Lesson 21, "Using XOAD," we will look into an Ajax framework that uses an alternative approach—the server-side, PHP-based XOAD.

LESSON 21
Using XOAD

In this lesson you will learn about XOAD, a server-side framework with Ajax support written by Stanimir Angeloff.

Introducing XOAD

So far in this part of the book we have looked at the prototype.js and Rico libraries and how they can help you to develop Ajax applications. Unlike these client-side libraries, which are written in JavaScript, XOAD is a *server-side* Ajax toolkit written in PHP.

This lesson discusses some of the concepts behind XOAD and the basics of its use.

> **Tip** *XOAD* is an acronym for *XMLHTTP Object-oriented Application Development.*

All our work so far has concentrated on the use of JavaScript to handle both the server request and the returned data in Ajax applications. XOAD is a server-based solution written in PHP that takes a slightly different approach.

XOAD applications make server-based PHP functions available to the client-side JavaScript interpreter by passing serialized versions of them as JavaScript objects.

> **Note** Under the hood, XOAD employs JSON (JavaScript Object Notation) for communications. JSON was described in Lesson 19, "The prototype.js Toolkit."

Downloading and Installing XOAD

XOAD is made up of many PHP and supporting scripts and can be down-loaded as an archive file from http://sourceforge.net/projects/xoad. To install XOAD successfully, you need FTP access to a web server that supports PHP and (to use the more advanced features of XOAD) the MySQL database. Detailed instructions for installing XOAD can be found in the downloaded material, and there is a public forum at http://forums.xoad.org/.

A Simple XOAD Page

Let's take a look at an example of the simplest XOAD page. Suppose that you have a PHP class that you want to use in your XOAD application. This class is stored in the PHP file myClass.class.php:

```php
<?php
class myClass {
  function stLength($mystring) {
      return strlen($mystring);
    }
  function xoadGetMeta() {
      XOAD_Client::mapMethods($this, array('stLength'));
      XOAD_Client::publicMethods($this, array('stLength'));
    }
}
?>
```

This simple class has only one function, stLength(), which merely returns the length of a string variable. We also added some *metadata* to the class in the form of the function xoadGetMeta(). This information tells XOAD which methods from the class are available to be exported to the main application. In this case there is just one, stLength().

> **Caution**   It is not absolutely necessary to include metadata in the class, but it is recommended. Without metadata, all methods will be public, and method names will be converted to lowercase.

Now you need to start constructing the main application script xoad.php.

> **Tip**   The Ajax applications developed in previous
> lessons were HTML files with file extensions .htm or
> .html. Because our XOAD application contains PHP
> code, it must have a suitable file extension. Most web
> server and PHP implementations will accept a file
> extension of .php, and some will allow other exten-
> sions such as .php4 or .phtml.

Listing 21.1 shows the XOAD application. This is a fairly pointless pro-
gram that simply returns the length of a string, "My XOAD Application".
Nevertheless, it demonstrates the concept of methods from server-side
PHP classes being made available on the client side as JavaScript objects.

LISTING 21.1   A Simple XOAD Application

```php
<?php
require_once('myClass.class.php');
require_once('xoad.php');
XOAD_Server::allowClasses('myClass');
if (XOAD_Server::runServer()) {
  exit;
  }
?>
<?= XOAD_Utilities::header('.') ?>
<script type="text/javascript">
var myobj = <?= XOAD_Client::register(new myClass()) ?>;
var mystring = 'My XOAD Application';
myobj.onStLengthError = function(error) {
  alert(error.message);
  return true;
  }
myobj.stLength(mystring, function(result) {
  document.write('String: ' + mystring
➥ + '<br />Length: ' + result);
  });
</script>
```

On loading the preceding document into a browser, the page simply says:

```
String: My XOAD Application
Length: 19
```

I won't go into much detail about how the PHP code works; this is after all a book about Ajax, not advanced PHP. It's important, though, to understand the concepts that underpin the code, so let's step through Listing 21.1 and try to understand what's happening:

```php
<?php
require_once('myClass.class.php');
require_once('xoad.php');
XOAD_Server::allowClasses('myClass');
if (XOAD_Server::runServer()) {
  exit;
  }
?>
<?= XOAD_Utilities::header('.') ?>
```

The first part of the script includes both xoad.php and the required class file myClass.class.php, and informs XOAD which classes it may access (in this case only one).

The XOAD function runServer() checks whether the XOAD request is a client callback, and if so handles it appropriately. The header() function is used to register the client header files.

Now let's look at the remainder of the script:

```javascript
<script type="text/javascript">
var myobj = <?= XOAD_Client::register(new myClass()) ?>;
var mystring = 'My XOAD Application';
myobj.onStLengthError = function(error) {
  alert(error.message);
  return true;
  }
myobj.stLength(mystring, function(result) {
  document.write('String: ' + mystring
➥+ '<br />Length: ' + result);
  });
</script>
```

See how the remainder of the script is a <script>...</script> element? The line

```javascript
var myobj = <?= XOAD_Client::register(new myClass()) ?>;
```

exports the public methods declared in myClass.class.php to a JavaScript object. We now have a JavaScript object with a method stLength() that allows us to use the method of the same name from the PHP class myClass.

XOAD HTML

XOAD HTML is an extension that allows for the easy updating of HTML page elements using XOAD. The following examples show the use of the `XOAD_HTML::getElementByID()` and `XOAD_HTML::getElementsByTagName()` methods, which do exactly the same thing as their equivalent JavaScript DOM methods.

XOAD_HTML::getElementById()

You will recognize the layout of the code in Listing 21.2 as being similar in structure to the basic XOAD program discussed earlier.

Rather than include an external class file, in this example we have defined a class, `Updater`, within the application itself. The class contains a single function, `change()`.

The first line in that function uses `XOAD_HTML::getElementById()` to identify the page element with and ID of `display`. Subsequent program lines proceed to change the text and background color of the page element.

The function `change()` is made available as a method of the JavaScript object `myobj` and can then be called like any other JavaScript method:

```
<a href="#server" onclick="myobj.change();
return false;">Change It!</a>
```

Figure 21.1 shows the program's operation.

LISTING 21.2   Application to Use `XOAD_HTML::getElementById`

```php
<?php
class Updater
{
    function change()
    {
      $mytext =& XOAD_HTML::getElementById('display');
      $mytext->style['backgroundColor'] = 'yellow';
      $mytext->innerHTML = 'My background
 color has changed.';
    }
}
define('XOAD_AUTOHANDLE', true);
```

continues

LISTING 21.2   Continued

```
require_once('xoad.php');
?>
<?= XOAD_Utilities::header('.') ?>
<div id="display">My background color is white.</div>
<script type="text/javascript">
var myobj = <?= XOAD_Client::register(new Updater()) ?>;
</script>
<a href="#server" onclick="myobj.change();
➥return false;">Change It!</a>
```

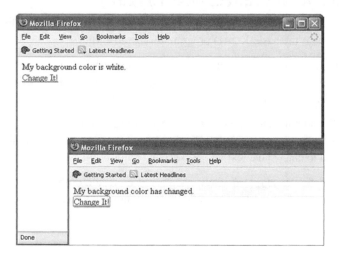

FIGURE 21.1   Using XOAD_HTML::getElementById().

XOAD_HTML::getElementsByTagName()

The XOAD_HTML::getElementsByTagName() method, like its JavaScript equivalent, returns an array of elements with a certain element type. Listing 21.3 identifies all page elements of type <div> and changes some of their style attributes.

LISTING 21.3   Changing All Page Elements of a Given Type

```php
<?php
class Updater
{
    function change()
    {
        $mydivs =& XOAD_HTML::getElementsByTagName('div');
        $mydivs->style['height'] = '60';
        $mydivs->style['width'] = '350';
        $mydivs->style['backgroundColor'] = 'lightgreen';
      $mydivs->innerHTML =
➡'Size and color changed by XOAD';
    }
}
define('XOAD_AUTOHANDLE', true);
require_once('xoad.php');
?>
<?= XOAD_Utilities::header('.') ?>
<script type="text/javascript">
var myobj = <?= XOAD_Client::register(new Updater()) ?>;
</script>
<style>
div {
border:1px solid black;
height:80;
width:150
}
</style>
<div>Div 1</div>
<br />
<div>Div 2</div>
<br />
<div>Div 3</div>
<a href="#server" onclick="myobj.change();
➡return false;">Update All Divs</a>
```

The three <div> elements in the page are identified by
XOAD_HTML::getElementsByTagName() and have their styles and sizes
changed.

Figure 21.2 shows the program in operation.

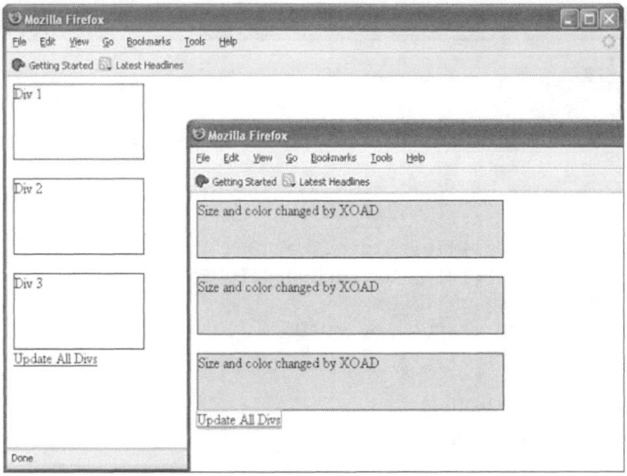

FIGURE 21.2   Selecting multiple page elements with XOAD_HTML.

> ![tip icon] **Tip**   XOAD_HTML has many other capabilities. Details of all the functions available within XOAD_HTML are in the XOAD download.

Advanced Programming with XOAD

XOAD has a range of advanced capabilities over and above those discussed in this lesson. In case you want to investigate the limits of what is possible using XOAD, here is an overview of the currently supported techniques.

XOAD Events

The XOAD framework also has support for *events*. A XOAD event instigated on one client's computer can be stored on the server and subsequently detected by other clients, making it possible to build complex applications in which users can interact. Such applications might, for instance, include chat, groupware, or similar collaborative tools.

Cache Handling with XOAD

XOAD allows for the caching on the server using the XOAD_Cache class. Caching results gives significant performance improvements, especially when server-side routines are time-intensive (such as sorting a large data set or performing queries on a sizeable database table).

XOAD Controls

You can define custom client controls in XOAD using the XOAD_Controls class.

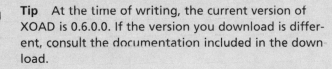

Tip   At the time of writing, the current version of XOAD is 0.6.0.0. If the version you download is different, consult the documentation included in the download.

Summary

This lesson examined a server-side implementation of an Ajax toolkit, in the form of XOAD.

XOAD allows the methods contained within PHP classes stored on the server to be made available to client programs using JavaScript. This forms an interesting contrast in approach compared to the client-side techniques discussed in Lessons 19 and 20.

This concludes Part IV of the book and, in fact, the book itself. You should now have a good understanding of Ajax application architecture and the coding techniques on which it is based.

Good luck with your experiments in Ajax!

INDEX

launching, 100-101
myAJAXlib.js, 180
RSS headline readers, 153-154
callRICO() function, 206
center tags (HTML), 22
CERN (Conseil Europeen pour le
Recherche Nucleaire), Internet development, 6
change() function, 219
character strings, split() method, 130
charAt method, responseText property,
105
child nodes, adding DOM to, 144-145
childNodes property, 147
cinematic effects (Rico), 213
client-server interactions, 70-71
client-side programming, defining, 11
code, platform tests, troubleshooting, 189
color (HTML), 19
comments (HTML), 18
constructors, creating instances, 81
CreateAttribute method, 147
CreateElement() method, 146-147
CreateTextNode() method, 144, 147

D – E

date() command (PHP), 57
DELETE requests, 159-160
developer's tokens, 162
<div> containers, 116
DNS (Domain Name Service) servers, 11
doAjax function, 178-182
DOCTYPE declarations (XML), 64-65
DOCTYPE elements, 16
document elements (XML), 63
DOM (Document Object Model), 81-82
    appendChild() method, 144
    child nodes, adding to, 144-145
    createElement() method, 146
    createTextNode() method, 144
    document methods table, 147
    elements, deleting, 153
    getAttribute method, 69
    getElementByID method, 143
    getElementsByTagName method, 143
    node methods table, 147
    node properties table, 147
    nodes, 67-68

tagname properties, 68
text properties, 69
DTD (Document Type Definitions), 64

ELEMENT declarations (XML), 65
email, Internet development, 5
Engines (Ajax), 73
error handling
    application design, 190
    Back button codes, 184
    bookmarks, 185-186
    browser caches, 191
    code, platform tests, 189
    GET requests, 191-192
    JavaScript libraries, 183
    links, 185-186
    page design, 188
    Permission Denied errors, 191
    POST requests, 191-192
    security, 189
    spiders, 187
    unsupported browsers, 186-187
    user feedback, 186
eval() function, JavaScript libraries,
177-179
event handlers, 42
    basic application creation example,
    117-118
    JavaScript functions, calling, 48-49
    myAJAXlib.js, calls for, 180
    onChange event handler, 49
    onClick event handler, 43-44, 49
    onLoad event handler, 49
    onMouseOut event handler, 49
    onMouseOver event handler, 46-49
    onSubmit event handler, 49-51

F – G

feedback (user)
    basic application creation example,
    120-121
    JavaScript libraries, 182
    server requests, 109-110
    troubleshooting, 186
file extensions, PHP files, 54
firstChild property, 147
for loops, 59
Form objects, 195-196
form tags (HTML), 31-33
form validation example (JavaScript),
    51-52